— YORKSHIRE —
Literary Landscapes

PAUL CHRYSTAL

DestinWorld
publishing

First published 2018
Destinworld Publishing Ltd
www.destinworld.com

British Library Cataloguing in Publication Data.
A catalogue record for this book is available from the British Library.

ISBN 978 1 9997175 7 5

Cover design by Ken Leeder

Printed and bound in Bulgaria pulsioprint.co.uk

To John Hogg, my Latin teacher at Hartlepool Grammar School who showed me that there was a lot more to poetry and prose than just words on a page.

Contents

Acknowledgements

Thanks to Dr Sophie Bowness of the Hepworth Estate for permission to use the images of Barbara Hepworth, originally published in Dr Bowness' *Barbara Hepworth and the Yorkshire Landscape* (2003). Thanks to David Gooderson for permission to include the excerpt from his play *War! Lies! And a Packet of Fags* in the chapter on 'Woodbine Willie', taken, almost verbatim, from a speech he made in Central Hall, Westminster, on Armistice Day, 1921. Thanks, too, to Adrian Mealing, agent for Ian McMillan, for permission to use extracts from his poetry. The photograph on p. 69 comes courtesy of Sarah Sheils of the Mount School and author of *Among Friends* in which the image was first published.

Introduction

As the title suggests, this book describes and depicts how various Yorkshire landscapes have influenced the work of a selection of Yorkshire writers. I use the term 'landscape' in its broadest sense, to include urban, industrial, social and cultural, skyscapes and seascapes, as well as the more usual rural. 'Yorkshire' is the county before the 1974 reorganisation, so this permits us to include Thornaby and Middlesbrough; 'Yorkshire' also embraces writers born here or who lived here and whose work has been influenced by Yorkshire landscapes of one sort or another. 'Literary' takes in novelists, poets, playwrights and social commentators. Such extravagant licence, then, results in a book that includes fifty or so writers in at least as many locations, stretching from Swaledale in the north to Barnsley in the south, from east coast Scarborough and Whitby to Clapham in the western Dales. The writers are as ancient as seventeenth-century Andrew Marvell and as modern as 2017 debut novelist Fiona Mozley.

'Landscape' of one kind or another, of course, features prominently in a lot of English literature: Hardy's Wessex, Wordsworth's and the other Lake Poets' Lake District, Austen's Steventon and elegant Bath, Lawrence's well-mined Nottinghamshire, Robert Robert's and Walter Greenwood's Salford slums, and Auden's north Pennines are obvious examples. But Yorkshire, it may surprise some to know, can easily out-landscape all of these places with a plethora of *literati*, all describing industrial, social, cultural, urban and rural landscapes, along with a number of seascapes.

Of course, the literary landscapes of Yorkshire encompass much, much more than the Brontë country that many assume accounts for the totality of northern landscapes as portrayed in northern literature; moreover, there is much more here than the clichéd, 'grim-up northness' that even today exposes the lazy stereotyper who writes off the 'gritty' north simply as a blasted heath above Haworth. The landscapes of Yorkshire have inspired and motivated many of the writers in this book to challenge and change that indolent, incomplete perception.

So, allow *Yorkshire Literary Landscapes* to take you on a not always so grim and gritty northern odyssey, encompassing all that is good in landscape-inspired Yorkshire writing. Hopefully, the book will excite in many readers their innate sense of place, it will shine light on the topographies and landscapes that inspired the writers and thus enhance the enjoyment and understanding of you, their readers, of their works and these places. At its simplest level, a writer's place of birth and the circumstances into which she or he is born, their education, family, local topography, environment and employment can offer different but associated landscapes that conspire to inform the writer's work. On a more complex level, socio-economic factors, politics and chance add different layers to the landscapes at any writer's disposal. The modest aim of this book is help to elucidate and illuminate some of those various landscapes.

For a number of reasons the book can only be selective in terms of the writers included; for each it offers only a glimpse into what is a huge subject. Hopefully, though, it will inspire and entice you to find out more about the writers and their landscapes, and perhaps visit and experience at first hand just what it was that informs and forms their writings.

Paul Chrystal
York 2018

The stunning hills above Marsden.

Simon Armitage (b. 1963)

We also pass a farmer in his yard, power-washing a donkey with a high-pressure hose.

Simon Armitage, *Walking Home: A Poet's Journey*

Simon Armitage was born in Marsden, a village near Huddersfield, and still lives in the area; he is currently a Professor of Poetry at the University of Sheffield. Marsden is the last word in refreshing eccentricity and culture: Marsden Cuckoo Day offers clog dancing, a duck race, a procession and a 'cuckoo walk'. The Marsden Jazz Festival comes round every October, and the Imbolc Festival celebrates the 'triumph of the Green Man' and the victory of spring over winter, as represented by Jack Frost, complete with fire juggling and giant puppets. The Mikron Theatre Company lives here; its website describes it as the world's only professional theatre company to tour by narrowboat; the narrowboat in question is the *Tyseley*, built in 1936 for the Grand Union Canal Carrying Company. In 2015 they performed in 150 venues:

> We have performed at allotments, care homes, community centres, dry docks, festivals, pubs, rallies, restaurants and village halls. We've even performed inside a tunnel, in the bows of a docked boat and in people's very own front rooms.

> [https://mikron.org.uk/about/]

The 'Cuckoo Day festival' takes its name from a local legend of the Marsden Cuckoo:

> Many years ago the people of Marsden were aware that when the cuckoo arrived, so did the Spring and sunshine. They tried to keep Spring forever, by building a tower around the Cuckoo. Unfortunately, as the last stones were about to be laid, away flew the cuckoo. If only they'd built the tower one layer higher. As the legend says, it 'were nobbut just wun course too low'.

> ['Marsden Cuckoo Festival preview',
> *The Huddersfield Daily Examiner*, 22 April 2010]

Such wonderful local events must have influenced Simon Armitage as he grew up surrounded by the awe-inspiring fells and dales. The local landscapes inform his poetry and imbue his travelogue books – both in their different ways exhibit the effect dramatic scenery (urban and rural) has on his writing.

For example, *Saturday Night* (1996) is a fifty-minute poetic commentary to a documentary about nightlife in Leeds. In 2010, Armitage walked his 'troubadour journey' – the 264-mile Pennine Way – giving poetry readings, often in exchange for donations of money, board and lodge; *Walking Home: Travels with a Troubadour on the Pennine Way* (2012) describes that journey.

Marsden today.

Between 2010 and 2012 Simon Armitage worked on the Stanza Stones project, a sequence of poems inspired by the Pennine Watershed and the relationship between the landscape and Yorkshire dialect: *In Memory of Water* (2013) comprises the different forms of water: Rain, Mist, Snow, Dew, Beck and Puddle. Simon's collaborators in this site-specific poetry were Tom Lonsdale and letter-carver Pip Hall: she located six secluded sites and etched his poems into stone to reflect the dramatic landscape all around that is indicative of the relentless environmental changes and weathering. The poem carvings can be found at six sites along the Pennines between Marsden and Ilkley, now known as the forty-five mile Stanza Stones Trail. The seventh stone remains undiscovered.

In 2012 the poet told the BBC:

> I think at some level for me it's about giving poetry back to the landscape…this is a county which is steeped in literary history and a lot of that is to do with the land, the geology, the environment and I think over the years I have taken from that. Now I want to give something back.

All Points North (2009) charts the poet's formative years, growing up in the north of England. His 'The Making of the English Landscape' (nodding to W. G. Hoskins' classic work) says it all: it is a poem in which he eschews tawdry football shirt collections and four-lane motorways for ditches, walls, sheep trails, middens, drove roads and burial mounds.

Fryup Dale, winter by Will Taylor. © Mercer Art Gallery, Harrogate.

J. C. Atkinson (1814–1900)

Before me, looking westward, was moor, so that I could see nothing else. On either side was moor with a valley on the left...across the valley was moor again...while behind me, as I knew, lay three good miles of moor, and nothing but moor...it was a wild as well as lonely solitude.

J. C. Atkinson, on first seeing the moors around Danby in 1850, in *Countryman on the Moors*, p. 13

Two miles outside Danby in Danby Dale is St Hilda's church. John Christopher Atkinson is buried there – ornithologist, natural historian and author of *Forty Years in a Moorland Parish: Reminiscences and Researches in Danby in Cleveland* (1891) in which he meticulously describes the 70,000 miles he is said to have covered hiking the North York Moors over fifty years.

Danby Parish Church around 1900.

North York Moors folk about the same time.

He was born in Goldhanger, Essex, and went to St John's College, Cambridge. After brief appointments in Herefordshire and Scarborough, Atkinson was presented with the living of Danby, and was vicar there for fifty-three years and, from 1891, a Canon of York Minster. He married three times and fathered thirteen children.

Atkinson pursued other interests, including folklore, vernacular architecture, and archaeology. His prolific publishing output includes *Walks, Talks, Travels and Exploits of Two Schoolboys* (1859), *British Birds' Eggs and Nests* (1861), *Sketches in Natural History* (1861), *A Glossary of the Cleveland Dialect* (1868), *The History of Cleveland, Ancient and Modern* (1872), *The Whitby Chartulary* (1879–81), *North Yorkshire Quarter Sessions Records* (ed., 1883, 1892), *The Chartulary of Rievaulx Abbey* (1889), *Scenes in Fairyland* (1892), and *Memorials of Old Whitby* (1894).

This extract from Atkinson's obituary published in the *Whitby Gazette* [6 April 1900, p. 8] encapsulates the life lived by the man as he traversed the moors in pursuit of his ecclesiastical duties or his personal research:

> A single visit to a parishioner would sometimes mean a walk of five miles, for his church stood isolated among the fields, and not more than 40 people lived within mile of it. Every Sunday he took two services and had to walk at least seven miles, while sometimes he did ten. To quote an admirer of Canon Atkinson who contributed to the Sunday at Home early in 1894, the result of interview –

> Canon Atkinson was a desperit fresh man ov 'is age. He will be 80 in May, but looks, talks, and works like a man ten or fifteen years younger. 'You see that hill,' he said, pointing to the brown ridge that shuts in the valley on the east. 'I go over that hill every Sunday afternoon to Fryup, and it's two-and-a-half miles the straightest way I can go – across fields and over walls and hedges.' There is a mission chapel at Fryup and another at Castleton, a large village to the west. These, with the parish church, make three pulpits the vicar and his curate have to fill every Sunday.

Detail from David Cox's *Crossing the Moor*, 1851;
City of Manchester Art Galleries.

Forty Years in a Moorland Parish reveals Atkinson's love of nature and of the far-flung parish in which he so assiduously worked. The vivid descriptions of moorland life are matched with conversations with moorland folk, most of whom would never have set foot out of the hills and dales. He describes the 'wild, solitary tracks and the deep pitches and steep ravine banks' over which an eagle might still be seen; chapters include a description of Danby in 1850; witches; The Wise Man or wizard; barrow-digging and archaeology; graves; winter on the moors and dogs in church and the dog-whipper.

Some Danby dialect recorded in *Forty Years in a Moorland Parish*:

- 'He's ower mickle a feeal to ken how many beans mak's five.' *He's tight-fisted.*

- 'He's that thin, he's lahk a ha'porth o' soap efter a lang day's weshing.' *He's skinny.*

- 'Ay, she's tied a knot with her tongue she'll be matched to unloose wiv her teeath.' *A woman newly married, but not wisely.*

- 'Ay, there's t'heead an' t' hair; but there's nowght else.' *(S)he's a bit thick.*

York's ancient Stonegate about 1890. It hasn't changed that much.

Kate Atkinson (b. 1951)

Amelia envisaged that between York and the royal-infested Scottish Highlands there was a grimy wasteland of derelict cranes and abandoned mills and betrayed, yet still staunch, people. Oh and moorland, of course, vast tracts of brooding landscape under lowering skies, and across this heath strode brooding, lowering men intent on reaching their ancestral houses, where they were going to fling open doors and castigate orphaned yet resolute governesses.

Kate Atkinson, *Case Histories*

Kate Atkinson was born in York into a family that ran a medical supply shop, and it is in that city that her first novel, *Behind the Scenes at the Museum* (1995), is set. The chief character is Ruby Lennox, a middle-class York girl living in the shadow of the Minster; the book traces Ruby's life, interspersed with flashbacks in which the lives of six generations of women from Ruby's great-grandmother Alice to Ruby's mother are narrated. The museum in question is York Castle Museum, which famously includes Kirkgate – a reconstruction of a Victorian street with old houses from the city, similar to the one in which Ruby's family lived. York history permeates the book: Laurence Sterne is there writing *Tristram Shandy*, the plashing of Viking oars can be heard still; 'the first printers and stained-glass craftsmen that filled the windows of the city with coloured lights' and a Roman army files past while Patricia and Ruby sip tea. All these evoke the city's Roman and Viking antecedents; its former pre-eminence as a publishing and printing city and the unsurpassed wealth of medieval stained glass in the Minster and in other churches. Sterne had close associations with York Minster and nearby Sutton-on-the-Forest, Stillington and Coxwold.

Stonegate in 2017. 'The Shop is in one of the ancient streets that cower beneath the looming dominance of York Minster' [*Behind the Scenes at the Museum*, p. 14]

In 2008, Kate Atkinson told *The Guardian* how *Behind the Scenes* came about, and York's starring role in it:

> First, the title. I had a dream in the early stages of writing the book…I was in the Castle Museum in York, on my own, in the middle of the night. Although it was dark and frightening, I was compelled to investigate (as we are in dreams) and, as I moved from room to room in the museum, objects sprang into life – a fire suddenly flared in a hearth, an automaton began to move.
>
> When I woke up I immediately thought, 'that dream was called Behind the Scenes at the Museum'. My second thought was more revelatory: 'Of course, that's what the novel should be called.' Looking at Behind the Scenes now, I can see that York, not Ruby, is the all-pervading main character of this book. The novel is a hymn to my relationship with the city, constructed out of history, memory and nostalgia.

I doubt it was incidental that the Castle Museum provided the backdrop for this dream. I visited it regularly from an early age, walking with my father from our shop, which, like the Lennoxes' shop that rose from the ashes of the Great Pet Shop Fire, sold medical and surgical supplies and was similarly located in Stonegate, the old Roman Via Pretoria stretching from the river to the headquarters of the Ninth Legion, now buried beneath the Minster. That walk took us through ancient streets so freighted with history that they can barely carry the burden. My father knew every shortcut there was, and those secret snickets and alleyways are an old and familiar groove in my brain.

The museum was a place of miracles and wonders for me, where the rooms and streets of the past were brought to life in a way that was (and still is) thrilling. My imagination was undoubtedly nurtured by those visits; in fact I am sure that they helped to build the foundations of my becoming a writer.

The Castle Museum illuminated.

One of the exhibits in the museum – a 1960s sitting room.

Alan Ayckbourn (b. 1939)

Most of my plays at some level are autobiographical

Alan Ayckbourn in an interview, 2012

Alan Ayckbourn was born in Hampstead; after school he took several temporary jobs, one of which was at the Scarborough Library Theatre, where he met the artistic director, Stephen Joseph, who later became his mentor and father figure and is founder of the UK's first modern professional theatre-in-the-round company. The Library Theatre was the predecessor of today's Stephen Joseph Theatre located in the former Odeon.

The Guardian (Monday 27 June 2011) uncovers one nugget of information relating to the effect of Scarborough on the playwright, suggesting that life in the town has added an acuity to his observations:

> His regional base is reckoned to have given edge to his observation, although life in Scarborough is not always quiet. Ayckbourn recently mistook a burglar in his home for one of his regular flow of visitors, and was caught up in a brief but passionate debate over whether his theatre was as important as threatened local public lavatories.

The Five Lamps, Thornaby.

Pat Barker (b. 1943)

By the late 1980s Barker had published three highly praised novels, but she was pigeonholed as northern, working-class, feminist and gritty. 'It's difficult to deny any of that, but it's not saying anything perceptive. You get to the point where people are reading the label instead of the book.'

**Pat Barker talking to Maya Jaggi in *The Guardian*,
16 August 2003**

Pat Barker was born into a working class family in Millbank Lane in Thornaby-on-Tees, the child of a drunken one night stand, after which Pat Barker was passed off as her mother's sister and her father an RAF pilot who never existed. Barker's grandmother, Alice, and step-grandfather, William, provided a home, initially on a chicken farm, until her mother married and moved out when Barker was seven; Barker stayed with her grandmother 'because of love of her' and a reciprocated dislike for her stepfather.

Later, the fish and chip shop her grandparents ran failed, leaving the family 'poor as church mice; we were living on National Assistance – "on the pancrack", as my grandmother called it' (*Sunday Times*, 1 July 2007). The experiences on the chicken farm were to reverberate sickeningly in *Blow Your House Down*. The chip shop banter between the customers and their battered lives informed and honed Barker's ear for regional dialogue, acerbic wit, punctured dreams and crucial social survival skills; the newspaper wrappings that Barker read in between customers provided the current affairs while the local library introduced her to Dostoyevsky, tempered by 'a lot of trash'.

Things could only get better, and so it was that Barker won a place at King James's Grammar School in relatively upmarket Knaresborough and then Grangefield Grammar School in more convenient Stockton-on-Tees. Barker went on to read International History at the London School of Economics from 1962–1965 and then returned to Thornaby to nurse her grandmother, who died in 1971. In doing so she becomes another example of what Richard Hoggart in *Uses of Literacy* calls a 'revisitor' – those propelled out of working-class poverty and cultural restriction through the grammar school system. Steven in *Lisa's England* and Colin in *The Man who Wasn't There* (1988) are later revisitors.

Barker is, of course, best known for her *Regeneration Trilogy* (1991–1995), but it is her earlier work, the regional novels, where we find landscapes from her early life breaking through. That said, even Billy Prior, the protagonist of the *Regeneration* trilogy, comes from the north-east of England in novels largely set in London, Scotland and France.

Union Street (1982) was to be her first published novel: seven stories woven together about English working class women whose lives are characterised by poverty, domestic violence, including rape, as they try to adapt to the industrial decay and dereliction besetting 1970s northern England. Ten years after the writing and after many a rejection (because it was 'bleak and depressing') Barker met novelist Angela Carter in 1978 at a writers' workshop. Carter was impressed and told Barker 'if they can't sympathise with the women you're creating, then sod their fucking luck', advising her 'to find the voices and social terrain of the working class culture she grew up in' (*Guardian*, 15 October 2003). Carter recommended she send the manuscript to Virago: *Union Street* remains one of their best-selling titles.

In what has been called 'Pat Barker's other trilogy' [by Belinda Webb, 20 November 2007 in *The Guardian*/Books Blog], *Union Street* was joined by *Blow Your House Down* (1984) and *Liza's England* (1986; originally published as *The Century's Daughter*). All three tracked the lives of working-class women in north Yorkshire. *Blow Your House Down* describes prostitutes living in a north of England city, who are stalked by a serial killer. Shades of the Yorkshire Ripper here, the man who haunted Yorkshire women of Barker's generation for years yet, as she points out, no one else really bothered about it until a middle class woman was murdered and eviscerated. *Liza's England*, hailed by the *Sunday Times* as a 'modern-day masterpiece', traces the life of a working-class woman born in the early 20th century.

Victoria Bridge over the Tees, seen from Thornaby.

The depressing urban wastelands that Barker was familiar with in and around Thornaby and Middlesbrough perfuse these three novels. However, there are glimmers of light in later work such as *Border Crossing* (2001) where the wastelands are beginning to benefit from regeneration. This dichotomy is a result of a number of factors amongst which is that Barker still lives in the north-east (Durham now) and she 'loves the local landscape: "Everything's deep in coal dust, and half a mile down the road there are cornfields"' [Maya Jaggi, *The Guardian*, 16 August 2003].

Horbury Bridge.

Stan Barstow (1928–2011)

The world may be full of fourth-rate writers but it's also full of fourth-rate readers.

Stan Barstow

Stan Barstow was born in the railway town Horbury, near Wakefield, the son of a coal miner. Barstow went to Ossett Grammar School, between Dewsbury and Wakefield, and then in 1944 took work as a draftsman and salesman for an engineering company. He is best known for his novel *A Kind of Loving* (1960), which has been translated into a film, a television series, a radio play and a stage play. Other novels include *Ask Me Tomorrow* (1962), *The Watchers on the Shore* (1966) in which Vic takes leave of the north and his wife for London bohemia; and *The Right True End* (1976). Barstow lived in Yorkshire most of his life, including a spell in Haworth.

When his father died in 1958 Barstow inherited his moped and drove around industrial West Yorkshire 'noting changes and collecting features' for Cressley, the fictional Yorkshire town he had plans to write about. He based Cressley on Dewsbury rather than Wakefield because he much preferred the stone of the former to the brick of the latter. He describes in his autobiography his early life growing up among what he later termed 'the lace curtain' working class, big on thrift and self-respect – 'poverty but not squalor'. Barstow's father sported a bowler hat and spats for special occasions. His mother wore a fox-fur 'complete with head' to Sunday chapel. His father topped up his wages by performing on the cornet with local brass bands; in *A Kind of Loving* Vic Brown's father played the trombone in pit bands. The house is utterly 'unlettered'.

This is an example, from Barstow's *In My Own Good Time*, of the environment in which Barstow grew up and which later informed his work:

> I can locate the warm heart of my childhood in the big family parties that my grandparents held at Christmas. How many there were I can't now say, and perhaps one very successful one, with a score or more relatives crammed into the small cottage, has left its happiness like a stain on my memory ever since. My mother's family were no strangers to rancour and bitterness: they bore lingering grudges against their own, and I recall that one of my aunts refused to speak to my mother for years. But none of that marred my pleasure in those get-togethers when, in the roasting heat of two huge fires, the square table in one room would be laden with all the good things of high tea, and games in the other would reduce the womenfolk and the children to helpless laughter. In that room also I would see my first dead body when my grandfather lay in his open coffin.
>
> My mother's thrift was a powerful factor in keeping us afloat, and other people's deprivation could sometimes surprise even her. She told of once going to visit my father's half-sister in Darton, a mining village near Barnsley. They had just finished their Sunday dinner when there was a knock on the door. A small boy stood there with a message: 'Me mam says can we borrow your joint.' The joint was tolerantly handed over and brought back a little later minus the slices with which the neighbours had made their meal.

A Kind of Loving was the first book in a trilogy, published over sixteen years, which followed Victor Brown through marriage, divorce and a relocation from the mining town of Cressley to London. The other two parts are *The Watchers on the Shore* and *The Right True End*. To make Vic more plausible and reachable Barstow wrote the book in the first person 'in a vernacular made up of West Riding idioms, Hollywood slang, and words and phrases brought back from overseas by returning servicemen'. He also deployed the historic present because 'that is what you use in Yorkshire for telling stories'. Barstow describes this device in his autobiographical *In My Own Good Time*:

> I would let Vic tell his story in the historic present rather than in the more customary past tense. Many people around me would relate events in the historic present (though, like the man who was surprised to be told he habitually spoke in prose, they didn't know they were doing it): 'I'm walking along Market Street when I catch sight of him coming round the corner. I can't get out of his way so I put a bold face on it and wait and see what he'll do …' It heightens the immediacy. You are there, even though what's being described has already taken place.

Horbury High Street.

Twenty-year old Vic Brown is a working-class Yorkshire man painfully inching his way up from his working class roots to a white-collar job via grammar school. When he gets typing pool girl Ingrid Rothwell pregnant, all that changes: Vic is horrified at the prospect of being trapped in dull Cressley. He is forced not only to marry Ingrid, whom he does not love, but also to move in with his mother-in-law due to a local housing shortage. Tedium soon plagues the marriage, leaving Vic to discover what love and being in love really are. What is required is grown-up compromise, adaptability and finding the right kind of loving.

The novel is the first of a number of mid twentieth-century books in which, in a time of immense social and cultural change, the themes of social mobility rising from working class to middle class, social isolation and the desire to improve one's lot with education and then escaping the trap that is the dreary north, as it is perceived, are given free rein. Barstow himself calls this a 'provincial renaissance too strong to be denied', having bought and read Keith Waterhouse's *Billy Liar*, Len Doherty's Sheffield-based *The Good Lion*, and the novels of John Braine and Nottingham's Alan Sillitoe.

The River Tees around the time of Bell's research.

Lady Florence Bell (1851–1930)

The north shore, the Durham side [of the Tees], is even more desolate than the other, since it has left the town behind, and the furnaces and chimneys of the works are interspersed with great black wastes, black roads, gaunt wooden palings, blocks of cottages, railway lines crossing the roads.

Florence Bell, *At the Works*

Florence Bell was the stepmother of Gertrude Bell; the family lived in Coatham, now part of Redcar. Bell was much more than just the wife of ironfounder Sir Hugh Bell; as a social investigator of some note, she is the author of *At the Works* – a perceptive, detailed social study of Middlesbrough as a manufacturing town over thirty years, published in 1907. One of the significant findings was that in over one-third of the houses visited, the wife did not know what their husbands' wages were. However, in the remainder, while the man of the family was the undisputed breadwinner, many well-run families owed everything to the household and its financial management that was exclusively the domain of the wife and mother. It is she who allocated the contents of the pay packet and ran the house.

Bell and her fellow researchers (all women) visited over 1,000 families connected with the steel industry from 1880 or so to 1906 to produce this fascinating and revealing work of social history. The aim, successfully achieved, was to describe the daily lives of the workmen engaged in the iron trade, living in crowded conditions in small, cheap houses in the 'mean streets of Middlesbrough' with their families, which could just as likely include up to twelve children rather than the two or three the houses were built for. Although Bell paints a bleak, realistic, landscape, she is sure that there can be hope:

> There is nothing to appeal to a sense of art and beauty... But yet imagination can be stirred – must be stirred – by the Titanic industry with which it deals, by the hardy, strenuous life of the north, the seething vitality of enterprise with which the town began... towards the centre and the north, serried together in and out of the better quarters, there are hundreds of the little streets we have described, in which lives a struggling, striving, crowded population of workmen and their families: some of them, as will be shown, prospering, anchored, tolerably secure, some in poverty and want, the great majority on the borderland between the two.

> [*At the Works*, p. 7]

Ladles in the steelworks.

Steelworkers knocking off under the Tees Transporter Bridge.

Her description of the industrial banks of the Tees reveals a squalid landscape:

> the banks on either side are clad in black and grey. Their aspect from the deck of the ferry-boat is stern, mysterious, forbidding: hoardings, poles, chimneys, scaffoldings, cranes, dredging-machines, sheds. The north shore, the Durham side, is even more desolate than the other, since it has left the town behind, and the furnaces and chimneys of the works are interspersed with great black wastes, black roads, gaunt wooden palings, blocks of cottages, railway lines crossing the roads and suggesting the ever-present danger, and the ever-necessary vigilance required in the walk from the boat. A dusty, wild, wide space on which the road abuts, flanked by the row of the great furnaces, a space in which engines are going to and fro, more lines to cross, more dangers to avoid; a wind-swept expanse, near to which lie a few straggling rows of cottages. A colony of workmen live here.

[*At the Works*, p. 14]

Poverty in the back streets of Middlesbrough.

Surely, no more than would be expected of an unremittingly industrial landscape. Bell herself confesses that many of the inhabitants love living in these circumstances, driven more by the sense of community they inspire than by natural beauty.

City Hall, Leeds 1911 – later to inspire Bennett with its classical concerts.

Alan Bennett (b. 1934)

We started off trying to set up a small anarchist community, but people wouldn't obey the rules.

Alan Bennett

Auden it was, 'quacking' at the dons in the refectory in Exeter College Oxford in 1955, who nearly scuppered Alan Bennett's early ambitions to be a writer:

> so when Auden outlined what he took to be the prerequisites of a literary life, or at any rate a life devoted to poetry, I was properly dismayed. Besides favourite books, essential seemed to be a literary landscape (Leeds?), a knowledge of metre and scansion and (this was the clincher) a passion for the Icelandic sagas. If writing meant passing this kind of kit inspection, I'd better forget it.

[*The Guardian*, 8 November 2009]

Despite eschewing the importance or influence of a 'literary landscape', to a large degree Alan Bennett's early days in Armley, Leeds, define the man and inform much of his work. His regular forays over forty years to his house in the Dales village of Clapham further reinforce his associations with Yorkshire and add a rural landscape to the decidedly urban, working class and back-to-back backdrop that is Armley. Taken together, the rural and the urban merge to provide an influence that is unmistakably Yorkshire, with characters that are often decidedly northern, if not specifically Yorkshire, folk. His uncanny ear for Yorkshire dialect, the absurd and just plain daft things people sometimes say, office gossip minutiae, and the eccentricities of the ordinary man and woman is unmatched. His mother ('Mam') is a source of some of this with such axiomatic jewels as, on the trouble with being bald, 'You'd never know where to stop washing your face' – a gift that he elsewhere described as 'an unerring grasp of inessentials which is the prerogative of mothers'.

Michael Brooke captured the essence of Bennett's writing very well when he wrote:

> with family life either fractious or awkwardly silent, his elderly characters often facing a lonely, neglected death. His ability to get under the skin of such withdrawn people and write about them with such empathy, compassion and wry (often gallows) humour makes him not just a great writer but the definitive chronicler of a certain kind of English ordinariness, whose outwardly placid surface conceals inner turmoil as intense as anything displayed by the more emotionally articulate.

[http://www.screenonline.org.uk/people/id/504794/]

Armley is famous for two very different things: the forbidding Armley Gaol and the friendly Alan Bennett. Alan Bennett grew up in the Leeds suburb before going to Oxford in 1954; his father was a violin-playing butcher, his mother, Lilian Mary Peel, was a housewife who sadly suffered from depression and Alzheimer's later in life. He attended Leeds Modern School, now Lawnswood School in Otley Road, where a plaque proudly proclaims that their library is named after him. Nothing could be more fitting, as it was the public library in Armley that provided the boyhood Bennett with an early, unshakeable grounding in reading, books and an enduring and acute observation of characters – Armley-type characters – their foibles and their exquisite mundanities.

Armley Library – another source of inspiration.

In 2011 Bennett took a small, albeit influential step in repaying his debt to the council-run Armley library when he spoke in support of keeping the Kensal Rise library open – local to where he now lives in north London. Kensal Rise closed despite Alan Bennett's efforts: 'Libraries have to be local; the early part of a child's reading life is vital.' He knew that that was true from personal experience, just as it was true for hundreds of other writers including, for example, Laurie Lee, who 'gorged' on Joyce and Huxley at Stroud public library [*The Telegraph*, 15 October 2011]. Bennett has famously said [in *The London Review of Books*, 33(15), · 28 July 2011 pp. 3–7] that 'Having learned to read there was nothing in the house on which to practise my newly acquired skill.' And so Armley public library then became an obligatory weekly outing for Mr and Mrs Bennett and their two sons. An early favourite was the Dr Dolittle stories of Hugh Lofting and Richmal Crompton's Just William books.

One of Bennett's earliest descriptions of Leeds finds him saying 'like the other great Northern cities still intact in 1951, but though I was not blind to its architectural splendours, unfashionable though at that time they were, it was a soot-blackened, wholly 19th-century city' [*London Review of Books*, 36 (12), 19 June 2014, pp. 29–30]. Leeds, then, was formative but never the be-all-and-end-all. Bennett, it seems, was bursting to get out. We read that he can forlornly remember 'a time when I thought my only connection with the literary world would be that I had once delivered meat to TS Eliot's mother-in-law' [*The Guardian*, Thursday 7 May 2009].

A murky Leeds day just after the war in 1945.

In the same article he recalls how a trip to Haworth parsonage was ruined for his mother by the scruffiness of the Brontës' decor: 'the fireplace wanted blackleading and the curtains were a disgrace. "Too busy writing their books to keep the place up to scratch."'

Yorkshire is by no means everywhere in Bennett's work but it is all over the place. *The History Boys* is set in a boys' grammar school in Sheffield in 1983 where eight students have just obtained the school's highest ever A-level scores and are hoping to go to Oxford or Cambridge by taking the entrance exam in history. His first television play, *A Day Out* (1972) and then *Sunset Across the Bay* (1975) see Bennett plundering his Yorkshire heritage in descriptions of a Halifax cycling club on a day out in 1911, and an elderly couple, based on his parents, retiring to Morecambe but feeling homesick for 'mucky' Leeds. In 1984, *A Private Function* is set in the post-war Yorkshire of his youth with food rationing and unlicensed pig smuggling. *Talking Heads* references Harrogate and Bettys Café.

> *People* [2012] is set in South Yorkshire although Bennett admits the inspiration was the former stately home of Temple Newsam in Leeds. 'It was the only museum open during the war and I thought it was a wonderful place.'
>
> [*Yorkshire Life*, 15 August 2013]

The monologue *Hymn* and *Cocktail Sticks*, is a 2012 duet of autobiographical plays about Bennett's childhood in Leeds. *Hymn* is about a pivotal event in Bennett's youth when his musical father (who, suitably attired, played along to the Palm Court orchestra on the radio) tried to teach him the violin. When Bennett fails he achingly realises that his father's disappointment 'will outlast the violin and my childhood, and go down to the grave'. Along the way it evokes another key influence on Bennett's early life in Leeds in much the same way as did Armley library: concerts at Leeds Town Hall inculcated a lasting love for classical music. *Cocktails Sticks* resumes the family memoir and the descriptions of his Leeds childhood, first published in his *A Life Like Other People's* (2009).

Richard Hoggart's *The Uses of Literacy* (1957) had an important influence on Bennett – providing a simultaneous literary and urban landscape all of its own; he confides to having first read it in New York in 1963

> not out of any sociological interest but from homesickness… for me the book was a taste of Yorkshire and more particularly of Leeds. It wasn't the Leeds I knew. We lived in Armley which had some slums but was otherwise boring and comparatively genteel. Hoggart's Leeds was Hunslet, poorer, slummier…Before I read *The Uses of Literacy* had I had any thoughts of writing, my childhood – safe, dull and in a loving family – was enough to discourage me. My life, it seemed to me, was not conducive to literature, but it was reading Hoggart's close account of his growing up in Hunslet that changed my mind.

> [*Keeping On Keeping On*, 2016, p. 341]

Alan Bennett is much, much more than the font of classic one-liners; yet he is the master of pithy wit, much of which was honed in and mined from his early Armley life; here are more delicious Bennett quotations:

- The closing of public libraries is a form of child abuse' [in the sense that it damages a child and hinders it].

- Overheard being uttered by English tourists in Luxor: 'Palm trees are nothing to us – we're from Torquay.'

- All you need to do if you want the nation's press camped out on your doorstep is to say you once had a wank in 1947.

  [*The Guardian*, 8 November 2009]

- We have fish and chips, which W. and I fetch from the shop in Settle market-place. Some local boys come in and there is a bit of chat between them and the fish-fryer about whether the kestrel under the counter is for sale.…Only when I mention it to W. does he explain Kestrel is now a lager. I imagine the future is going to contain an increasing number of incidents like this, culminating with a man in a white coat saying to one kindly, 'And now can you tell me the name of the Prime Minister?'

[*Writing Home*, 1994, diary entry for 25 July 1985, p. 144]

- What I'm above all primarily concerned with is the substance of life, the pith of reality. If I had to sum up my work, I suppose that's it really: I'm taking the pith out of reality.

- On being asked by Sir Ian McKellen in 1997 whether he was gay or straight: 'That's a bit like asking a man crawling across the Sahara whether he would prefer Perrier or Malvern water.'

- At eighty, things do not occur; they recur.

[*The Uncommon Reader*, 2007]

- History is just one fucking thing after another.

[*The History Boys*, 2004]

- History is a commentary on the various and continuing incapabilities of men. What is history? History is women following behind with the bucket.

- Definition of a classic: a book everyone is assumed to have read and often thinks they have.

- Mark my words. When a society has to resort to the lavatory for its humour, the writing is on the wall.

[*Forty Years On*, 1968]

- It was the kind of library he had only read about in books.

[*The Uncommon Reader*, 2007]

- If you find yourself born in Barnsley and then set your sights on being Virginia Woolf, it's not going to be roses all the way.

[*Writing Home* 1994]

Phyllis Bentley above the industrial landscape of Halifax.

Phyllis Bentley (1894–1977)

Two strong passions have always ruled my life: The first is literature; the second is the West Riding.

Phyllis Bentley

Phyllis Bentley was the youngest child of a Halifax mill owner at Dunkirk Mills; she was educated at Halifax High School for Girls and Cheltenham Ladies' College where she took an external London University degree in English and Mathematics. World War I saw her working at the Ministry for Munitions. In 1918, she went back to Halifax where she taught English and Latin at Heath Grammar School.

When it comes to literary landscapes – urban, industrial and rural – Bentley speaks eloquently for herself; this in an interview in the 1960s:

> I was a Yorkshire girl and proud of it. I loved the hills rolling away into the distance, springing out of each other in complex folds which, as it were, smiled sardonically at my efforts to find a word to describe them. I loved the purple heather and the dark rock, the russet bracken, the tumbling streams, the tough pale grass, the rough mortarless walls. Above all I loved the strong west winds, driving the great grey clouds relentlessly across the sky.

And this in the *Yorkshire Post* in 1935 – 'The Yorkshire I Know':

> My Yorkshire was called Halifax and Hebden Bridge, Sowerby Bridge, Norland, Barkisland, Huddersfield, Beacon Hill and Queensbury formed its uttermost boundaries. It was thus entirely occupied by spurs of the Pennine Chain, and those words Pennine Chain were magical ones to me... From my childhood upwards I was extremely proud of the geography and geology of the West Riding, long before I understood its significance in West Riding life. I was proud that my Yorkshire was coloured so richly brown on the map, and felt a genuine pity for children whose birthplaces were merely honey-coloured, or even, poor things, green: to live amidst gradients less exciting than my own seemed feeble. A true patriot, I adored even the inconvenience of my native land. That its contours were dangerous for bicycles, wore out horses, and necessitated numerous tunnels on the railway lines, seemed to me essentially right and proper. I loved to hear how the very tram lines had a narrower gauge in Halifax than elsewhere, because it had been thought impossible for any but single-decker trams to dare our preposterously steep streets. .... At night these trams lighted, crawling indomitably their dark appointed hills, traced beautiful changing patterns of diamonds and black velvet; to me they were symbols of that sturdy Yorkshire character I admired so much. Which stood no nonsense from anything, even gradients.

No doubt, the experience she got from voluntary work at the Halifax Child Welfare Clinic contributed to her sympathetic treatment of poverty in her work.

A prolific writer, she wrote novels, children's books and non-fiction works on the Brontës and the regional novel, short stories and a film script. She started as a novelist in 1918 but it was only after six unsuccessful novels and a collection of short stories that she found success in 1932 with *Inheritance*, lauded as the best regional novel since Thomas Hardy's Wessex books.

Inheritance has its roots in the stories her mother told her, especially those about her two uncles, Joshua and James Hanson – a typical West Yorkshire story of a powerful family riven by politics, by art, and by money. Joshua and James had taken two very different paths in life: Joseph stayed in textiles while James had given himself to education, became a political radical, set up a left wing newspaper and reformed the secondary schools of Bradford.

The saga continues with *The Rise of Henry Morcar* (1946) and *A Man of His Time* (1966). More landscape features in most of her twenty-one novels and the twenty-five other works, not least her 1962 autobiography *O Dreams O Destinations*; *The Brontës and Their World* (1969); *The Pennine Weaver* (1970) and in a short story collection: *Tales of West Riding* (1974).

The *Inheritance* trilogy is set in and around the Colne Valley and the textile workers who toiled there. The Ire Valley is the Colne Valley; Marthwaite, the main location, is Marsden; Annotsfield corresponds to Huddersfield; Hudley is Halifax; Ashworth is Bradford with elements of Halifax.

Halifax roots and a deep sense of the importance of local landscapes ensured that Bentley was eminently well-qualified to write the script for *We of the West Riding – The Life of a Typical Yorkshire Family* – an important 1945 British Council movie that was part of the 'Films of Britain 1947–50' series designed to boost morale in post-war Britain by depicting community spirit right throughout the land, and not just in London and the home counties. Bentley's landscapes are evident throughout the film:

Exploring the mill towns and textile industry within this area of Northern England, the film examines the structure of family life away from the British capital. Observed through the eyes of a little boy, he recounts visiting his family members who are all employed in different sectors of the local cloth industry. Much attention is paid to the dramatic rural landscapes and moorland that have become the focus for some of Britain's most renowned works of literature…

making sure that Britain is not depicted as 'London-centric' and values as well the diverse contributions to Britishness supplied by the far reaches of the country. It is a way of showing these differing areas in a positive light, diverting away from an idea that rural areas are somehow regressive. Highlight the fact that even though country lifestyles are perhaps different to those of people living in larger cities, there remain core values predicated on the importance of family, community spirit and supporting a greater ideal of Britishness.

[http://timeimage.wikispaces.com/We+of+the+West+Riding]

Along the way we discover the workers and the working practices in the local textile mills, and the leisure activities, which include football, pigeon-keeping, brass bands (there is footage of the Black Dyke Mills Band), amateur dramatics and cycling through the spectacular scenery. Singing is particularly important: the film ends with the traditional annual performance of Handel's *Messiah* by the Huddersfield Choral Society and the Holme Valley Male Choir.

Edmund Bogg (1851–1931)

T'owd Chief

Edmund Bogg, writer, rambler and bohemian, founded the Leeds Savage Club around 1891. When 'T'owd Chief' was not busy rambling or travelling around Yorkshire, armed to the teeth with sketch pads, pencils and notebooks rather than bows and arrows, he was hard at work penning one of his many excellent books on his beloved Yorkshire countryside, books for which he is still justly remembered today.

Bogg came from the Wolds hamlet of Duggleby where his father was a wheelwright. Schooling was in short supply as was, presumably, action of any sort and so, when he was twenty, he went to Leeds in search of work, which he found in joinery and then as a 'colourman', mixing paints for artists. The bohemian artists he met appealed and he, combining both of his new skills, set up in business as a picture dealer and framer with a gallery and workshop in Woodhouse Lane, living nearby with his wife, Fanny, and their young family. In due course he attracted a coterie of young artists (including, for example, Owen Bowen) whom he paid to go off to paint in the countryside and bring back to Leeds artworks he could sell in his shop.

Leeds Savage Club, modelled on the Savage Club in London (founded in 1857 and still one of the leading bohemian gentleman's clubs in London) brought together Leeds artists, musicians and writers in a bohemian, eccentric spirit as a refuge from the stiff and restricting everyday world. Membership was restricted to only fifty members who were called Savages, with a Chief as president, a Scribe as secretary, and Braves as committee men. The native Indian theme was Edmund Bogg's idea and he was duly elected Chief, to preside in feathers and war-paint over the usually boisterous pow-wows in the Wigwam, fuelled by firewater (whisky punch).

For Bogg, books came next. In 1892 he published *A Thousand Miles in Wharfedale and the Basin of the Wharfe* in which he describes a journey accompanied by his artist friends, full of florid descriptions of village and countryside, historical snippets, and wonderful illustrations courtesy of fellow travellers like Percy Robinson and Gilbert Foster, along with his own photographs. Its success led to *Edenvale to the Plain of York Or, a Thousand Miles in the Valleys of the Nidd and Yore*, followed by *A Thousand Miles of Wandering Along the Roman Wall, the Old Border Region, Lakeland, and Ribblesdale; Richmondshire and The Vale Of Mowbray; The Charm of the Hambletons Round About Thirsk, Coxwold, Kilburn, Byland And Rievaulx* and in 1902 the bestseller *Old Kingdom of Elmet*, which includes a description of Leeds around the turn of the twentieth century.

These books, given their subject matter, are, of course, the last word in literary – and urban – landscapes. Bogg died at his home in Caledonian Road, Leeds aged eighty-one. Characteristically, he wrote his own epitaph: it was time for him to 'bid adieu to the hills and vales, rivers and glens [and] glide gently down the river of life to journey's end, like the beautiful Wharfe'.

Barbara Taylor Bradford (b. 1933)

In my opinion, moderation is a vastly overrated virtue, particularly when applied to work.

Barbara Taylor Bradford, *A Woman of Substance*

Barbara Taylor Bradford was born, like Alan Bennett, in Armley, Leeds. The two went to the same infant school, Christ Church Elementary School, but neither can remember the other. She went on to Northcote Private School for Girls. Bradford is a prolific author having published thirty-five novels to date. Unit sales run into the tens of millions, so whatever anyone thinks about her work, she is eye-wateringly popular and has done immeasurable good for the book trade both in the UK, and around the world with her foreign language editions.

Bradford's first success came in 1979 when *A Woman of Substance* was a mighty multi-million selling success – one of the top-ten bestselling novels of all time. It tells the story of Emma Harte, a downtrodden Yorkshire housemaid who pulls herself together, gets her act together and accumulates huge wealth thanks to her amazing business skills, and, no doubt, her Yorkshire thrift. The posh and prestigious Marshall and Snelgrove department store that stood in Park Row Leeds is reinvented for *A Woman of Substance* as Harte Enterprises. Jenny Seagrove, Deborah Kerr and John Mills starred in a film version of *A Woman of Substance* with Brimham Rocks looming in the background in 1988. However, lengthy *Ravenscar Dynasty* (2006–2008) is not much about that place on the Yorkshire coast but rather the relationship between Edward IV and Richard Neville, the Earl of Warwick. Nevertheless, Patricia, her New York editor, is from Bridlington. You can take the Bradford out of Leeds, and Bradford can, and does, take the Leeds out of Bradford...

Grim and industrial Shipley.

John Braine (1922–1986)

> *To be shockingly original with your first novel, you don't have to discover a new technique: Simply write about people as they are and not as the predominantly liberal and humanist literary establishment believes that they ought to be.*

John Braine

John Braine, one of the so-called 'angry young men' of the fifties, was born in a pokey terraced house off Westgate in Bradford, and moved to Thackley when his father took a job at Esholt Sewage Works. Thackley was next door to grim and industrial Shipley, a Joe Lampton kind of town, 'where the snow seemed to turn black almost before it hit the ground'. After time spent as a junior salesman in Christopher Pratt's furniture shop and then as progress chaser at the Hepworth & Grandage piston factory, Braine worked as a library assistant in Bingley Library until 1942. He is most famous for his first novel, *Room at the Top* (1957), although he did write more, including *Life at the Top*, a sequel to *Room at the Top*; *The Crying Game* (1968) and *Writing a Novel* (1974), a guide for aspiring novelists.

Room At the Top, along with John Osborne's *Look Back In Anger*, Allan Sillitoe's *Saturday Night And Sunday Morning* and Shelagh Delaney's play *A Taste of Honey*, all became successful films and were together seen as a late fifties thing in which the problems shared by ordinary young people were laid bare: the dominant theme was frustration and anger at the lack of opportunity or social mobility for young working class people in a Britain where people still knew their place, not least in the back streets of northern industrial towns.

Titus Salt in nearby Saltaire; courtesy of Simon Palmer and Jonathan Silver.

Titus Salt in Saltaire; courtesy of Simon Palmer and Jonathan Silver.

Growing up in the bleakness of Thackley must surely have inspired and tinged the plot and themes to be found in *Room at the Top*. The anti-hero, Joe Lampton – war orphan and demobilised at the end of World War II – spent his POW days learning accountancy and, on returning to dreary Dufton, resolves to carve out a better life for himself – indeed, to Joe Lampton, the only way is up. A move to up-market Warley with a good job and prospects helps him on his journey and paves the way for his entry into the world of the middle classes.

Lampton, a ruthless social climber, lodges with the Thompsons, a middle-class couple living in the posh part of town, known as 'T'top' and takes a 'room at the top' there. Dufton is in the past, Warley is his future. Through the Thompsons he is introduced to the local amateur dramatic society where he meets Susan Brown, the only daughter of a very successful local businessman. Joe seduces Susan who falls pregnant; although Joe loves another woman, Alice Aisgil, his aim is to marry Susan in order to achieve his social aspirations, and to show the world that he can get the better of Jack Wales, the dashing young man and heir who is Susan's fiancé.

The 1959 film of the book, in particular, clearly highlights and compares the bleak urban landscape of Dufton – fifties Thackley – with the promise offered by Warley.

A suitably atmospheric Scarborough Castle.

Anne Brontë (1820–1849)

Anne's unhappy times at Blake Hall near Mirfield where she worked as a governess for the Ingham family in 1839 are vividly recalled in *Agnes Grey* (1847). The moors around Haworth are referenced in the opening paragraphs: 'What happy hours Mary [Agnes' sister] and I have past, while sitting at our work by the fire, or wandering on the heath-clad hills.' We see the homesickness and uplifting memories again in a poem in which Anne's feelings are vocalised by an orphan girl in 'Verses by Lady Geralda' (1836):

> Why, when I hear the stormy breath
> Of the wild winter wind
> Rushing o'er the mountain heath,
> Does sadness fill my mind?
>
> For long ago I loved to lie
> Upon the pathless moor,
> And hear the wild wind rushing by
> With never ceasing roar;

Its sound was music then to me;
Its wild and lofty voice
Made my heart beat exultingly
And my whole soul rejoice.

In 1840 Anne took up a second post as governess under the Reverend Edmund Robinson at Thorp Green Hall in the hamlet of Thorp Green near Little Ouseburn eight miles north-west of York. The house reappears as Horton Lodge in *Agnes Grey* where the hero was governess to the Murray children. During Anne's time at Thorp Green, she went with the family on their five-week annual holidays to Scarborough, a place she loved; the resort features in *Agnes Grey*'s final scenes and as Linden-Car village in *The Tenant of Wildfell Hall* (1848).

Anne wrote her poem 'Lines Composed in a Wood on a Windy Day' at Thorp Green in 1842, finally published in 1846 under her pen name, Acton Bell, and annotated in Anne's hand with 'Composed in the Long-Plantation [a wood near the Hall] on a wild bright windy day'. But it is a seascape, not a landscape, that we see in the poem. The references to the windswept sea and its uplifting force are no doubt inspired by her times at Scarborough, and her nostalgia for those visits:

My soul is awakened, my spirit is soaring
And carried aloft on the wings of the breeze;
For above and around me the wild wind is roaring,
Arousing to rapture the earth and the seas…

I wish I could see how the ocean is lashing
The foam of its billows to whirlwinds of spray;
I wish I could see how its proud waves are dashing,
And hear the wild roar of their thunder to-day!

In *The Tenant of Wildfell Hall* Anne takes up the controversial themes and the social and cultural landscapes that had offended so many in Emily's *Wuthering Heights*: violence, inebriation and conflict are laid bare, all based on the alarming and shabby treatment she received at Blake Hall, and on Bramwell, her dissolute brother.

Some scholars believe that Wildfell Hall is based on Ponden Hall, a farmhouse near Stanbury in West Yorkshire. Blake Hall at Mirfield, where, as we have seen, Anne worked as a governess, was the model for Grassdale Manor, Arthur Huntingdon's country seat.

The Withens, Haworth – Wuthering Heights?

Charlotte Brontë (1816 –1855)

A landscape ceases to be topographical when there are people in it. When those people are the Brontë sisters, the landscape is far more than topographical. It becomes a literary landscape, but the literature cannot be fully appreciated without the topography, nor in the case of these sisters, something of their biography the Brontë novels are redolent of the moors that roll away from the bleak upland manufacturing village of Haworth.

Arthur Pollard in the Preface to his
The Landscape of the Brontës

The three Brontë sisters were born at 74 Market Street in Thornton on the edge of Bradford. In 1820 their father was appointed to the perpetual curacy in Haworth seven miles away and moved with the family into the five-roomed Haworth Parsonage. Countless books and articles have been written about landscape in the novels and poetry of the three Brontë sisters – and rightly so: the use of landscape in the Brontë books defines those books and their characters, and remains one of the reasons why they have enjoyed a wide appeal since publication. But there is much more to the Brontës' landscapes than that atmospheric blasted heath above Haworth…

Looming in the background to Charlotte Brontë's social novel, *Shirley* (1849), are the tempestuous 1811–1812 Luddite uprisings that beset the Yorkshire textile industry. Published under the pseudonym 'Currer Bell', the book is set around Birstall, some six miles south-west of Leeds; its main themes are industrial unrest and the role of women in society. So popular was the book that it became a popular girl's name; hitherto, Shirley was a boy's name. Settings in the book include the seventeenth-century Red House in Gomersal, Gothic Dewsbury Minster, Kirklees Hall, 'Nunnely Hall' in *Shirley*, and the Elizabethan Oakwell Hall, renamed 'Fieldhead' by Brontë and home to Shirley Keeldar – an orphaned heiress to a fortune, a self-assured, independent and determined young woman. When Charlotte Brontë visited her friend Ellen Nussey, a pupil at Oakwell, she took away memories that translated into:

> If Fieldhead had few other merits as a building, it might at least be termed picturesque: its irregular architecture, and the grey and mossy colouring communicated by time, gave it a just claim to this epithet. The old latticed windows, the stone porch, the walls, the roof, the chimney-stacks, were rich in crayon touches and sepia lights and shades. The trees behind were fine, bold, and spreading; the cedar on the lawn in front was grand, and the granite urns on the garden wall, the fretted arch of the gateway, were, for an artist, as the very desire of the eye.

> [*Shirley*, p. 193]

Elizabeth Gaskell described Oakwell, too, in her *The Life of Charlotte Brontë* (1857). The assault on Robert Moore's mill was based on the actual Luddite attack on Cartwright's Mill at Rawfolds. In *Shirley*, the family in Red House are the Yorkes and the house is renamed Briarmains.

Charlotte worked briefly as a governess at Stone Gappe in Lothersdale, near Skipton – the model for Gateshead Hall, the childhood home of the eponymous heroine of *Jane Eyre* (1847). *Jane Eyre* was also written under the pen name 'Currer Bell'. Much of the novel's action takes place in and around gothic Thornfield Hall – a thoroughly depressing place full of empty rooms and exuding an air of gloom and melancholy to match Mr Rochester's persistent low mood. Outside, though, the grounds were a much happier, uplifting place.

Controversy rages over the real-life location of Thornfield; Haddon Hall, near Bakewell, has staked a claim but it is much more likely to be one of three other places. It was possibly North Lees Hall in Hathersage just over the border from Yorkshire in Derbyshire, based on the fact that Morton in the novel is thought to be based on Hathersage, and that in 1845 Charlotte Brontë stayed at the Hathersage vicarage, visiting Ellen Nussey, whose brother was the vicar, while she was writing *Jane Eyre;* many of the locations in the novel mirror places in Hathersage. Or, High Sunderland Hall in Halifax, which is suitably gothic and was well known to the Brontë family; or Norton Conyers House near Ripon. The Clergy Daughter's School that Charlotte attended is reborn as Cowan Bridge's punitive and austere Lowood school in *Jane Eyre*.

The cluttered burial ground and the parsonage about 1910: 'a graveyard so filled with graves that the rank weed and coarse grass scarce had room to shoot up between the monuments'.

The burial ground in 2017.

Landscape is integral to the Brontë sisters themselves – it is in their DNA. As a young woman Charlotte went to work at Roe Head School between 1831 and 1832 and, even though away from Haworth, still reminisced on the Haworth landscape when, homesick, she heard the wind blow at Roe Head; it was the Haworth wind that was blowing:

> The wind pouring in impetuous current through the air, sounding wildly, unremittingly from hour to hour, deepening its tone as the night advances, coming not in gusts, but with a rapid gathering stormy swell. That wind I know is heard at this moment far away on the moors at Haworth. Branwell and Emily hear it, as it sweeps over our house, down the Churchyard and round the old church, they think perhaps of me and Anne.
>
> [*Jane Eyre*, as quoted in H. Hendrix, *Writers' Houses and the Making of Memory*, p.107]

And, as noted, it's not just the wind, it's the whole landscape that immerses and imbues. Charlotte writes in 1850:

> My sister Emily had a particular love for them [the moors], and there is not a knoll of heather, not a branch of fern, not a young bilberry leaf not a fluttering lark or linnet but reminds me of her. The distant prospects were Anne's delight, and when I look round, she is in the blue tints, the pale mists, the waves and shadows of the horizon. In the hill-country silence their poetry comes by lines and stanzas into my mind.

But it was not always fond memories of a Haworth heaven on earth. The following rather contradicts what Charlotte had written in the very same *Roe Head Journal* of 1831–1832 when describing Haworth, showing just how homesickness and time can dictate one's feelings and inject a dose of realism:

> no other landscape than a monotonous street – of moorland, a grey church tower, rising from the centre of a graveyard so filled with graves that the rank weed and coarse grass scarce had room to shoot up between the monuments.

Sentiments that we see again in her preface to sister Emily's *Wuthering Heights*, wondering why the complete strangers in the burgeoning tourist trade they had created had any interest in the 'wild moors of northern England'. Indeed, Elizabeth Gaskell concurred with these bleak comments on the bleak landscape when she wrote in her *Life of Charlotte Brontë* after an early autumn visit:

> It was a dull, drizzly Indian-inky day...lead coloured [passing] grey, dull-coloured rows of stone cottages...poor, hungry-looking fields; stone fences everywhere, and trees nowhere...moors everywhere above and beyond.

The moors above Haworth.

Emily Brontë (1818–1848)

Emily Brontë taught at Miss Patchett Ladies' Academy at Law House, near Halifax, for six months in 1837-1838. She later used her experiences here as a source for parts of her only novel, *Wuthering Heights* (1847), published under the pseudonym, Ellis Bell. If Dante Gabriel Rossetti is to be believed, the landscape created by Emily is nothing short of chthonic: 'A fiend of a book – an incredible monster [...] The action is laid in hell, – only it seems places and people have English names there' [Letters of Dante Gabriel Rossetti to William Allingham, 1854–1870]. While maybe not quite hell on earth, wild, bleak and desolate the setting for *Wuthering Heights* certainly is, and Brontë has drawn for us one of the greatest, most vivid landscapes in English literature, made all the more atmospheric and dramatic because it was there, all around her, tangible, dynamic and visible on her very doorstep at the Haworth parsonage.

Charlotte Brontë criticised Jane Austen's fiction for describing the nineteenth century equivalent of tidy and manicured suburbia: 'carefully-fenced, highly cultivated garden, with neat borders and delicate flowers' [letter of 12 January 1848 to George Lewes in response to his advice to her, after the publication of *Jane Eyre* to write less melodramatically, like Jane Austen]; the landscape we encounter in *Wuthering Heights* could not be more different. 'Nature', as Professor John Bowen points out in his *Walking the Landscape of Wuthering Heights*.

> is often deeply inhospitable in the book, not easily subdued to human purpose, comfort or design. Landscape is thus never simply a setting or something to be contemplated in Brontë's work, but an active and shaping presence in the lives of its characters.

> [www.bl.uk/romantics-and-victorians/articles/walking-the-landscape-of-wuthering-heights]

Rural landscape – as central as it to the book and to its characters' actions, moods and thoughts – is only one of the landscapes described by Emily. Domestic violence, addiction and mental illness reveal a social aspect integral to the industrial landscape that pervades the mill town down the hill from the parsonage; they create both a social and a cultural landscape, separate from but dependent on, the rural. And this, when viewed along with those glowering moors, only adds to the overall oppressive nature of the book's hinterland and influences how the characters behave.

Indeed, some of the contemporary reviewers picked up on this outrageous fusion. *The Examiner* (8 January 1848) believed the characters to be less civilised than the pre-Bronze Age Mycenaean Greeks: 'the people who make up the drama, which is tragic enough in its consequences, are savages ruder than those who lived before the days of Homer'. The *New Monthly Magazine* (January 1848) was equally appalled: the novel 'should have been called Withering Heights, for anything from which the mind and body would more instinctively shrink, than the mansion and its tenants, cannot be easily imagined… a perfect misanthropist's heaven'.

The book, then, its landscapes, its apparently rude middle class characters and their servants with their thick regional accents and the general 'grim-up-northness' – all this conspired to disturb the middle class sensitivities of the 'down south' press and their readerships, enabling reviewers to resort to stereotypes about life and people in the north of England.

But these reviewers, and others like them, miss the point entirely. Emily's aim was to challenge and disturb the comfortable and naïve assumptions about life and society which prevailed in environments and landscapes to be found in, for example, publishing houses in the capital and places like them. Charlotte defends the essential 'rustic' quality of Emily's work:

> [It is] rustic all through. It is moorish and wild and knotty as a root of heath. Nor was it natural that it should be otherwise; the author being herself a native and nursling of the moors…. Ellis Bell [Emily] did not describe as one who found pleasure in the prospect; her native hills were far more to her than a spectacle; they were what she lived in, and by, as much as the wild birds, their tenants, or as the heather, their produce. Her descriptions, then, of natural scenery, are what they should be, and all they should be.

The mystic quality, the desolation and the innate barrenness are palpable, as when, for example, Nelly flees Wuthering Heights,

> I bounded, leaped, and flew down the steep road [from Wuthering Heights]; then, quitting its windings, shot direct across the moor, rolling over banks, and wading through marshes: precipitating myself, in fact, towards the beacon-light of the Grange.

> [Chapter 17]

It is there when Cathy is sucked into a life of misery at the Heights, obsessed with Penistone Crags and its 'fairy cave' as described by Nelly:

> The abrupt descent of Penistone Crags particularly attracted her notice; especially when the setting sun shone on it and the topmost heights, and the whole extent of landscape

besides lay in shadow. I explained that they were bare masses of stone, with hardly enough earth in their clefts to nourish a stunted tree.

[Chapter 18]

However, the reviews quoted above take no account of this description Emily gives of the moors on a warm, sunny day when Cathy and Linton muse on what constitutes the perfect heaven: the landscape is by no means unremittingly bleak, here it is positively bucolic:

He said the pleasantest manner of spending a hot July day was lying from morning till evening on a bank of heath in the middle of the moors, with the bees humming dreamily about among the bloom, and the larks singing high up overhead, and the blue sky and bright sun shining steadily and cloudlessly. That was his most perfect idea of heaven's happiness: mine was rocking in a rustling green tree, with a west wind blowing, and bright white clouds flitting rapidly above; and not only larks, but throstles, and blackbirds, and linnets, and cuckoos pouring out music on every side, and the moors seen at a distance, broken into cool dusky dells; but close by great swells of long grass undulating in waves to the breeze; and woods and sounding water, and the whole world awake and wild with joy. He wanted all to lie in an ecstasy of peace; I wanted all to sparkle and dance in a glorious jubilee.

[Chapter 24]

Frances Hodgson Burnett (1849 –1924)

If you look the right way, you can see that the whole world is a garden.

Frances Hodgson Burnett, *The Secret Garden*

Born in York Street, Cheetham Hill, Manchester, Hodgson Burnett is remembered for three successful and popular novels for children: *Little Lord Fauntleroy* (1886), *A Little Princess* (1905), and *The Secret Garden* (1911). Frances was the middle child of five children of Edwin Hodgson, an ironmonger from Doncaster, and his wife, Eliza Boond, from a comfortable Manchester family. Frances' father owned a business in Deansgate, selling ironmongery and brasses.

The family was left without income when her father died of a stroke in 1852; in 1865 they all emigrated to Tennessee where Frances, aged nineteen, took up writing, publishing stories in magazines.

Outdoor space, books, gardens and flowers were always important to Burnett: in 1852 the family had moved to a more spacious newly built house opposite St Luke's Church, with lots more outdoor space all around. When her father died Frances was looked after by her grandmother who bought her books and encouraged her reading, especially her first book, *The Flower Book*, full of coloured illustrations and poems. Reduced family income necessitated a move to industrial Salford where the Hodgsons lived with relatives in a house that boasted a large enclosed garden. Frances Hodgson Burnett was educated at first at a dame school where she first read a book about fairies. A further move involved a house with no flowers or gardens close to an area of extreme poverty. In 1870, her mother died, and in 1872 Frances married Swan Burnett, and lived in Paris for two years before returning to the United States to live in Washington, DC; Hodgson Burnett then turned her hand to novels. *Little Lord Fauntleroy* was published in 1886 and made her name. About this time she was regularly travelling back to England

and in the 1890s bought a house, where she wrote *The Secret Garden*.

Her first novel, *That Lass o' Lowrie's* (1877) is set in Lancashire. Her habit of curling her boys' long hair and dressing them in frilly tunics re-emerged in *Little Lord Fauntleroy*. Cedric, the hero, was modelled on Burnett's younger son, Vivian. From the mid-90s Burnett lived in Great Maytham Hall, Rolvenden, Kent. The walled gardens here and the abundant flowers provided the inspiration for *The Secret Garden*, which she wrote in the rose garden in 1904 after a spell in London and in Salford's Buile Hill Park. Maytham Hall became Misselthwaite Manor situated on a bleak moor somewhere in Yorkshire.

In a book full of stereotypical descriptions and statements about India and the Indian people, some of which today are considered decidedly racist, it is refreshing to read passages such as this:

> I just love [the moor]. It's none bare. It's covered wi' growin' things as smells sweet. It's fair lovely in spring an' summer when th' gorse an' broom an' heather's in flower. It smells o' honey an' there's such a lot o' fresh air—an' th' sky looks so high an' th' bees an' skylarks makes such a nice noise hummin' an' singin'. Eh! I wouldn't live away from th' moor for anythin'… Our Dickon goes off on th' moor by himself an' plays for hours. That's how he made friends with th' pony. He's got sheep on th' moor that knows him, an' birds as comes an' eats out of his hand. However little there is to eat, he always saves a bit o' his bread to coax his pets.

> [Chapter 4]

The Sowerby family – Dickon, and Martha, the speaker here – come over as true Yorkshire people with their broad Yorkshire accents, and love for the natural beauty of the flora and fauna of the Yorkshire landscape. A landscape that presumably derives from descriptions read rather than experienced first-hand by Burnett.

1993 saw a film adaptation with Maggie Smith as housekeeper, mean Mrs Medlock, set in the imposing Victorian Gothic Allerton Castle at Allerton Mauleverer near Knaresborough. Fountains Hall, the country house near Ripon was also used for some scenes.

Boggle Hole.

A. S. Byatt (b. 1936)

He [Ash] remembered most, when it was over, when time had run out, the day they had spent in a place called Boggle Hole, where they had gone because they liked the word.

A. S. Byatt, *Possession: A Romance*

Byatt grew up in the same clever, edgy household as her little sister, Margaret Drabble. She endured the same shouty, anxious mother (Kathleen, herself a Browning scholar and a trapped housewife), went to the same good Quaker school in York, The Mount, where they both endured the inconvenience of having their mother as one of their teachers, and went to the same Cambridge college – on the insistence of their mother – an alumnus of that very same college, Newnham. So far, so bad. It was only on Byatt's graduation that the two sisters' paths started to diverge and the long-running enmity (tedious to both when asked about it) between the two began to simmer. As a young woman Byatt confesses to a terror of the prospect of eternal domesticity – a terror replicated in one of the characters in her novel, *The Children's Book*, about which she says,

> represents my greatest terror which is simple domesticity. Yes. I had this image of coming out from under and seeing the light for a bit and then being shut in a kitchen, which I think happened to women of my generation.

> [*The Guardian*, 25 April 2009]

We can glimpse, then, the York domestic landscape occasionally glinting through; likewise the religious: while she may not espouse Quaker doctrine she has taken on board their meditative and contemplative strengths discovered at The Mount:

> I am not a Quaker, of course, because I'm anti-Christian and the Quakers are a form of Christianity but their religion is wonderful – you simply sat in silence and listened to the nature of things.

> [*The Guardian*, 25 April 2009]

This patient assessment, rational analysis, is a quality that has informed her writing ever since.

Yorkshire pervades the four books in Byatt's quartet about the members of a Yorkshire family: *The Virgin in the Garden* (1978), the first in a quartet that includes *Still Life* (1985), *Babel Tower* (1996) and *A Whistling Woman* (2002). Part of *The Virgin in the Garden* fictionalises Byatt's days at the Mount School when she attended reading circles set up by professor of English Literature, Philip Brockbank, at the University of York.

This Yorkshire family is used as a vehicle with which the author examines issues surrounding art, literature, religion, science and social change from around the accession of Elizabeth II in 1953 to the end of the 1960s. In the first book Byatt focuses on the three children of public schoolmaster Bill Potter: Stephanie, an English teacher; Frederica, a gifted intellectual; and Marcus, a boy with emotional issues. Although there are other dimensions to all three characters, Byatt's domestic landscape amongst the social realism is quite evident. The Potter girls both get to Cambridge University (as Byatt and her sister did) at a time when women undergraduates were considerably thin on the ground. Alongside this we are guests at a mock-Elizabethan pageant staged in the grounds of a stately home in North Yorkshire, Long Royston Hall.

In *Still Life* Byatt, covering 1954–1959, lays bare the dichotomy and conflict between unbridled ambition and constricting domesticity, confinement and self-fulfilment: Stephanie graduates to become a comfortable and secure housewife (Byatt's great fear), who misses her former intellectual life, while ambitious party-girl Frederica's marriage ends in divorce, propelling her into a new life as a resourceful single mother.

Babel Tower charts Frederica's new life in London with its intellectuals, bohemians, obscenity trial and free love – a universe away from Stephanie back in safe Yorkshire.

A Whistling Woman (…will always come to some bad) covers 1968 to 1970 with Frederica living it up now as a television host and published author. How very different then from life in Yorkshire, but no! The Yorkshire moors of Frederica's childhood have themselves become a hotbed of late sixties counterculture where Frederica's part-time lover, John Ottakar, is working in a kind of university (formerly Long Royston Hall) that becomes a hippyish anti-university, the new North Yorkshire University. Moreover, the moors are also home to an outlandish religious cult commune – the Quakerish Joyful Companions – populated by counter-culture characters (who would find a good home at Timothy Leary's Harvard), and led by Joshua Ramsden, a psychiatric patient.

In 1990 Byatt took time off from writing the quartet to publish *Possession: A Romance*. The exigencies of their research project lead academics Roland and Maud to Yorkshire in their pursuit of the Victorian poets Randolph Ash and Christabel LaMotte. Attracted by the place name Boggle Hole ('a nice word') Roland suggests a detour. Over 100 years before, Randolph Ash and Christabel LaMotte were themselves on the Yorkshire coast in 1860:

> He [Ash] remembered most, when it was over, when time had run out, the day they had spent in a place called Boggle Hole, where they had gone because they liked the word.

The reference to Boggle Hole must surely have been inspired by Byatt's memories of seaside family holidays in Filey as a young girl. Boggle Hole is a pretty inlet south of Robin Hood's Bay. A boggle is a local name for a hobgoblin, the 'little people' who lived in caves along this coast and in the more remote corners of the North York Moors. More prosaically Boggle Hole itself was where smugglers used to land their prodigious contraband.

Roland and Maud come to the conclusion that LaMotte's poem, 'Melusina', has got to be set in Yorkshire – 'it's full of local words from here, gills and riggs and ling…she talks about the air like summer colts playing on the moor. That's a Yorkshire saying' (p. 264). Arriving at Thomason Foss, the academics realise that this was part of the specific setting for 'Melusina'. Byatt is using a literary landscape of her own to illuminate the very same literary landscape deployed by Christabel LaMotte. This walk around Goathland and Mallyan Spout recreates a similar trek described by Ash in a letter at the beginning of Chapter 14 in which he mentions 'Eller Beck' and the wonderful, valley-deep 'Beck Holes'.

Beck Hole in 1903.

Mount girls doing fieldwork near Filey; courtesy of Sarah Sheils.

Len Doherty (1930–1983)

Sid Chaplin described Doherty as being part of a 'Northern writers' mafia' – responsible for kitchen sink/ angry young men literature of the period, including Chaplin, Barstow, Braine and Waterhouse.

Sid Chaplin

Len Doherty has been described as being 'among the most important practitioners of the socialist novel in Britain' (Philip Bounds, *Orwell and Marxism: The Political and Cultural Thinking of George Orwell*). He was born in working-class Maryhill, Glasgow, and moved with his family to Yorkshire in the 1940s, taking work as a miner at the age of seventeen. While working at Thurcroft Colliery near Rotherham, he joined the local Communist Party and was one of a number of working class writers of the period sponsored by the Party and published by Communist Party company Lawrence & Wishart. His first novel, *A Miner's Sons*, (1955) is acknowledged as one of the most successful socialist and social novels.

1957 saw publication of Doherty's second novel *The Man Beneath*; about the same time Doherty left the Communist Party and joined the staff of the *Sheffield Star*. His third novel, *The Good Lion,* was published in 1958 to critical acclaim. Here is the review in the conservative *Spectator* [3 October 1958, p. 38], alluding to the debt the book owes to Doherty's own experiences in the industrial landscapes around Sheffield:

> Len Doherty, the author of The Good Lion, is a Yorkshire miner, and this is his third book – a good one about working-class life. It is a straight, self-projecting account of a Bevin boy's first couple of years as a miner: the new digs, the progression through various jobs to work at the coal-face, evenings breaking up dance halls with the gang, boxing in a local contest, arguing with Communists, looking for a girl. Doherty springs no surprises and, one

imagines, keeps well within his own experiences, but his writing is hard and honest, and he describes action with unusual skill.

Sid Chaplin, the Durham-born miner and *Guardian* columnist, described Doherty as being part of a 'Northern writers' mafia' – responsible for kitchen sink/angry young men literature of the period, including Chaplin, Barstow, Braine and Waterhouse. Much of Doherty's work was focussed on the Party's mainly Leeds-based Yorkshire District Cultural Committee, giving lecturers at Leeds University.

On the beach at Scarborough, around 1910.

Margaret Drabble (b. 1939)

When I go back to Sheffield I feel very close to it –
although the whole family has moved away, there's
something about the people, about the manners that
I recognise.

Margaret Drabble

Drabble was born in Nether Edge, Sheffield, the second daughter of
lawyer and novelist John F. Drabble and the teacher and Newnham,
Cambridge, graduate Kathleen Marie (née Bloor). She is a younger
sister of the novelist and critic A. S. Byatt. After evacuation to
Pontefract, wartime bombing forced a prudent family relocation to
strategically less important York. Drabble, like her sister, was educated
at the prestigious Quaker Mount School at York, where her mother
was on the teaching staff; Judi Dench was a contemporary: Margaret
(fairy Moth), sister Susan (Hippolyta) and Judi Dench (Titania) all
performed together in *A Midsummer's Night Dream*. Drabble then

won a major scholarship to Newnham College, Cambridge, where she read English and gained a starred First. She joined the Royal Shakespeare Company at Stratford in 1960, but left to write.

1950s Sheffield.

When asked how much Yorkshire there is in her novels, Drabble's reply confirmed that the county of her birth and adolescence is very much in evidence, not least the landscapes of her youth:

> Has Yorkshire influenced your work?
>
> Very much so. I may have left when I was just 15, but I keep on returning, and finding much pleasure in my visits. A lot of 'Yorkshire landscapes' find their way into my work, and I think that my characters often look at things in a Yorkshire way. I still feel very Northern, and that's what counts.

> [*The Yorkshire Post*, 1 September 2009]

The interview goes on to elicit warm memories of happy days in Pontefract, youth hostelling around Kettlewell, Sunday lunch in one of the Dales' pubs, walking along a limestone edge, Conisbrough Castle, the setting of Scott's *Ivanhoe*, school trips to Rievaulx Abbey and the temples.

Scarborough in the early 1960s.

I used to love Filey and Scarborough as a child, we'd go to
posh Scarborough for a lunch or tea, and stay in a bed and
breakfast in Filey, and I adored walking along Filey Brigg. I
still do… it is a remarkable place.

[*The Yorkshire Post*, 1 September 2009]

Scarborough days are remembered in the short story, *A Pyrrhic
Victory* (1968) where a tough, hangover-plagued hill walk on Elba
rekindles Anne's memories of the family quarrels that broke out over
the choice of a picnic site. The colourful rock pools on the beach
reminded her, twelve years old, of the Scarborough equivalent, 'dark
and cold and grey':

What she had liked then had been the waves breaking in
great showers of spray on the rocks when the sea was rough:
a wild rough coast, but beautiful, and she would try to get
out near those mountains of water, she would try to get wet.

When asked to name her favourite Yorkshire author, Drabble said:

> JB Priestley – whose plays are still revived frequently, but whose books are not so popular as they were, which is a pity, because they are extraordinary writing by any standards. I am so delighted that English Journey has just been re-published this year...Priestley was an archetypal Yorkshireman, but also a citizen of the world.

> [*The Yorkshire Post*, 1 September 2009]

As of 2017 Drabble has published nineteen novels, the first, *A Summer Bird Cage*, came out in 1963. Her non-fiction work includes *A Writer's Britain: Landscape in Literature*. Her infamous long-running spat with sister A. S. Byatt is source of long-running tedium for both women. Drabble reveals (in the semi-autobiographical *The Pattern In The Carpet*, 2009) that its origins lie in the reference to a family tea service in one of Drabble's novels – a tea service that Byatt had her eyes on for use in one of her novels. Not only is this the storm in a teacup to end all teacup storms but it is a good example of how the domestic landscape, however trivial, can intrude on a writer's life and work.

Yorkshire, then, features in a number of Drabble's books, even if sometimes only in a tangential, routine autobiographical way. More blatant influences, however, include, for example, the heroine in *Jerusalem the Golden* (1967); Clara Maugham, the intelligent, attractive final-year London university student and middle of three sisters grew up in Yorkshire like Drabble. Clara's home, run by a dominating mother (Drabble had enduring issues with her difficult mother), was the suffocating, non-event Northam (a fictionalised Sheffield), which she escapes by virtue of the grammar school system and the NHS. Life in Northam – a metaphor for 'life up north' – has instilled in Clara a hatred of domesticity and small town mentality. As with so many of her literary contemporaries, down south London (golden Jerusalem), land of opportunities, has given her an escape route, but she wants and needs so much more still, 'the true thick brew of real passion'. Yorkshire is a contact point between Drabble and Clara but the bleak small town landscape and the emotionally arid and penurious family Clara endured could have little in common with

Drabble's comparatively comfortable York days. Nevertheless, Drabble was bursting to escape.

Dreary Northam resurfaces in the state-of-the-nation novel, *The Radiant Way*. Its function here is to characterise the (stereotypically) 1980s dead-end north – deprived, working class, 'grim-up-northness' – while London's Harley Street, with which the novel's action is shared and to where ambitious Liz has escaped, obviously represents the exciting, sophisticated and successful south, a land of opportunity, that golden Jerusalem but in which Blake's 'dark satanic mills' are conspicuously absent.

In the context of her northern upbringing, Drabble herself has said 'the Drabbles were boringly South Yorkshire' [*The Australian*, 1 February 2014]. In life and in *The Radiant Way*, she and Liz are in effect echoing the long tradition of a literary north–south divide portrayed in the industrial novel and championed by Gaskell in *North and South* (1855), Disraeli in *Sibyl* (1845), and, more recently and satirically, David Lodge in the University of Rummidge in *Nice Work* (1988). Growing up in Sheffield with its industrial landscapes and Blitz will have had a part to play in the experience; after Sheffield and Pontefract, York and Cambridge with their academia, elegance and refinements may well have given Drabble a taste of what was possible.

The setting for *The Sea Lady* (2006) is also inspired by the seascapes of Drabble's happy, month-long family holidays of her own childhood in the 1940s. Filey was the resort of choice with a month of ponies on the beach, picnics and long hours exploring rock pools or swimming. Drabble says:

> We first went there in 1946 or 1947, I had never seen the sea, and it was so wonderful that first time. My father was a barrister, then a circuit judge, and in Sheffield we hardly saw him. But in Filey we had his undivided attention. And my mother, who was solitary, depressed and angry at home, seemed to come out of herself when we were away.
>
> [*The Yorkshire Post*, 2 October 2006]

The Sea Lady tells how Ailsa and Humphrey, who met as children and later found each other again and married, travel to a fictitious north country coastal town thirty years after they divorced. Ailsa is a celebrity feminist, and Humphrey a prominent marine biologist. They are both to receive honorary degrees from a new university there. The novel reprises their lives thus far. Long before they were married they knew each other as children, in that same small northern seaside town, just after the end of the Second World War. The most vivid section of the story is the account of their childhood meeting and where Humphrey's two summers as a child in Ornemouth and Finsterness are described. At the end, swimming in the rock pool on the north east coast not only replicates the happy Drabble holidays but atones for the vandalism she wreaked on the rock pool in Elba in *A Pyhrrhic Victory*.

> When I go back to Sheffield I feel very close to it – although the whole family has moved away, there's something about the people, about the manners that I recognise.

[*The Guardian*, 17 June 2011]

Park Road at the top of Terry Street showing the type of houses that would have been in Terry Street; evidently not bin day.

Douglas Dunn (b. 1942)

A poet's cultural baggage and erudition can interfere with a poem.

Douglas Dunn

Scottish born poet Douglas Dunn was an undergraduate at Hull University, gained a First in English and in 1966 went on to work with Philip Larkin as a cataloguer at the Brynmor Jones Library until 1971. The office chat between the two was more often about jazz than poetry but Larkin did champion Dunn's work with Faber, his publisher. Dunn's poetry debut came in 1969 with *Terry Street*, a collection that described everyday life in an impoverished, working-class neighbourhood of Hull between Beverley Road and Pearson

Park. The inspiration and influence for this came from the one-up, one-down terraced house he and his first wife bought in Terry Street for £250.

In 1974 and 1975 he was writer in residence at the University of Hull. By the mid-1970s Dunn was at the centre of and mentor to a vibrant poetry scene in Hull. In 1982 he edited *A Rumoured City*, an anthology of work by writers associated with Hull, complete with a foreword by Larkin. Dunn's introduction to the collection highlights the frontier-like quality of life and versifying in Hull: '[it] detailed the poets' imaginative responses to a city with a peculiarly 'provisional, almost frontier quality' – something we shall hear more of when describing Larkin's work.

Dunn has said that 'Almost everything I have written has been dictated by something that has happened to me' [Guardian, 17 January 2003]; 'Terry Street' (ironically named in honour of Richard Terry – one of the earliest and most successful Baltic merchants in Hull) would seem to bear that out. There we observe, through Dunn's window on the Hull world, a mundane removal on a squeaky cart with the usual paraphernalia: mattress, cups, carpets, chairs, four Western paperbacks – and the unusual: a lawnmower – for there is no grass at all in Terry Street. In 'Men of Terry Street', Dunn introduces us to the shift workers: 'They come in at night, leave in the early morning. I hear their footsteps, the ticking of bicycle chains, Sudden blasts of motorcycles, whimpering of vans'. We meet the young women in rollers who scorn his culture – Mozart on Radio 3 – while he agonises over the rights and wrongs of social division. As a gang they boast 'they're not wearing knickers' but 'blush when they pass you alone'. The jocular Bobby on the beat, the sardonic bin men, the cheeky back-chatting urchins and the chewing-gum masticating young mothers are all there in Terry Street.

The poems inspired by Terry Street, the red-brick ('the colour of burnt carrots') bargain basement Hull hole with its outside loo and bijoux kitchen offer a graphic and realistic urban landscape – a landscape of poverty – that is second to none. Even the horses in 'The Horses in a Suburban Field', which encroaches on the rural, are held prisoner by the urban: they can't move without stepping over 'cans' or a 'bicycle frame'; the horses' pointless wandering 'through the dust' is just like 'the dead dreams of [Terry Street] housewives'.

Looking down Terry Street towards Beverley Road in 2017. The original terraced houses have been replaced with modern houses and a supermarket

Mill work in Leeds.

Isabella Ormston Ford
(1855–1924)

Justice is to be the foundation on which we must build, not the kind of justice we have hitherto considered for us, and which many countries pride themselves is their watchword and standard, but a justice that demands freedom for all.

Isabella Ormston Ford

Isabella Ford, social reformer, suffragist, socialist propagandist and writer, was born in St John's Hill, Clarendon Road, Headingley, Leeds, the youngest of eight children of Quakers Robert Lawson Ford and Hannah (née Pease). At the age of ten she lived in Adel Grange and from 1922 in a smaller property called Adel Willows.

While leafy Headingley may not have been a direct influence on her career and work, her father, a solicitor who also ran a local night school for mill-girls, certainly was. Indeed, the family generally, imbued with radical liberal politics and actively involved with the anti-slavery campaign, women's rights and humanitarian causes, was a major influence. Contact with the mill-girls gave Ford and her sisters a taste of working-class life and a view of the social and industrial landscape from which the mill-girls came from, as well as an acute insight into class inequalities, the plight of working-class women and a keen interest in the usually deplorable working conditions in the many mills in and around Leeds.

When Ford was sixteen, she took up teaching at her father's school. She also became a prolific public speaker and wrote pamphlets on socialism, feminism and workers' rights. The female mill workers she taught brought her into the trade union organisation in the 1880s; she became a member of the national administrative council of the Independent Labour Party and was the first woman to speak at a Labour Representation Committee (later the British Labour Party) when she took the stand at the conference in 1903. One of her aims in life was to focus on

> restoring life and happiness to women, a vast proportion of whom would never have required any such help if the conditions of their working lives, and especially their wages, had been such as to bring even the smallest amount of happiness or comfort within their reach.

> [*Women's Wages*, p. 4]

Ever at the cutting edge, Isabella Ford worked tirelessly amongst tailoresses who were campaigning for improved working conditions; in 1885, Isabella helped Emma Patterson, President of the Women's Protective and Provident League, to form a Machinists' Society for tailoresses in Leeds. This was the opening shot in a long campaign by Ford to improve the pay and conditions of women working in the textile industry in Leeds. In 1889 she established the Leeds Tailoresses' Union and the following year she was elected president. When this folded she established a Workwomen's Society, which was open to all women workers; she joined in the Tailoresses' strike in 1889 delivering speeches, organising the collection and distribution of relief, and publicising the strikers' cause in the press. The following year she marched with workers from Manningham Mills in Bradford and was subsequently elected a life member of the Leeds Trades and Labour Council. She was involved in the founding of the Leeds Independent Labour Party (ILP) and was elected president of the Leeds Tailoresses' Union. She sat on the executive committees of the National Administrative Council of the Independent Labour Party, the National Union of Women's Suffrage Societies, and the Women's International League for Peace and Freedom.

During the 1890s Isabella was active in propaganda work for the ILP all over the West Riding of Yorkshire, speaking 'often at street corners, in dingy club rooms, in hot, crowded school rooms' (*Bradford Pioneer*, July 1924); Adel Grange became a focus for anyone interested in socialism and women's rights, and drew in visitors from all social classes.

She was the author of numerous pamphlets, and wrote columns in *The Labour Leader*, *The Yorkshire Factory Times* and *The Leeds Forward*. From 1895 she was parish councillor for Adel-cum-Eccup. Her books include *Miss Blake of Monkshalton* (1890); *On the Threshold* (1895), which delineates competing socialist and feminist ideals and explores the opportunities open to women if they remained unmarried; *Mr Elliott* (1901); and *The Secret Diaries of Ciara Loughlin*. Pamphlets include *Women's Wages* (1893), *Industrial Women and How to Help Them* (1900) and *Women and Socialism* (1904).

Whitby in 2017.

Elizabeth Gaskell (1810–1865)

She set a whole novel on the North Yorkshire coast [Sylvia's Lovers] and although she only visited Whitby briefly for a fortnight in 1859, she seems to have some hereditary affinity with the landscape, so powerfully does she evoke it.

**Margaret Drabble, *A Writer's Britain:*
Landscape in Britain, p. 86**

Despite being born in the rarefied and relative luxury of a house in Chelsea's Lindsey Row (now 93 Cheyne Walk) Elizabeth Gaskell has a strong reputation for delineating northern industrial landscapes generally (not least in her *North and South*), and one Yorkshire landscape in particular – Whitby, where she sets *Sylvia's Lovers*. When her mother died she was sent to live with her aunt Hannah Lumb, in Knutsford, Cheshire, later to be immortalised as Cranford and Hollingford in *Wives and Daughters*. In 1832 Elizabeth married William Gaskell, the assistant minister at Cross Street Unitarian Chapel in Manchester, and moved with him to the city where the unremitting industrial surroundings started to exert an influence on Elizabeth's writing, informing her work in the industrial genre.

Gaskell's first novel, *Mary Barton: A Tale of Manchester Life* (1848) is set between 1839 and 1842 and tackles the difficulties faced by the Victorian working class, focusing on relations between employers and workers in Manchester. The preface exposes the compassion and empathy she had for the poor all around her:

> How deep might be the romance in the lives of some of those who elbowed me daily in the busy streets of the town in which I resided. I had always felt a deep sympathy with the careworn men, who looked as if doomed to struggle through their lives in strange alternations between work and want.

1855 saw the publication of *North and South*, in which Gaskell deploys a southerner from a cosy southern village to present and expatiate on the conflict between mill owners and workers in a city in the throes of industrialisation – namely, the fictional, smoggy industrial town of Milton, based on Manchester, which is in the textile-producing county of Darkshire. The heroine, Margaret Hale, fresh from the south, observes at first hand the harsh and unforgiving world born out of the Industrial Revolution as employers and workers clash in the first industrial strikes. *North and South* traces Hale's growing understanding of the complexity of labour relations.

Sylvia's Lovers (1863) opens in the 1790s in the coastal town of Monkshaven, for which Whitby, then a thriving Greenland whaling port, is the model. Press gangs are rife during the early years of the Napoleonic Wars. Sylvia Robson is living with her parents on a farm, loved by her somewhat boring Quaker cousin Philip Hepburn. Sylvia, however, meets and falls in love with Charlie Kinraid, a far more exciting prospect who is a whaling speksioneer (a chief harpooner, who is also in charge of cutting up the speck, or blubber, of the whale on a Whitby whaler); they get engaged, secretly. When Kinraid returns to his ship, he is, unfortunately, press-ganged away into the Royal Navy.

Gaskell's research for the book largely took the form of correspondence, not least with Dr William Scoresby, the famous Arctic explorer and former captain of a Whitby whaler. Scoresby was born in the village of Cropton twenty-six miles south of Whitby. This research obviously focussed on the eighteenth century and, more specifically, press gangs, Whitby and whaling. However, in 1859 she visited the town for a fortnight with her daughters Meta and Julia to see and experience the place for herself: a blue plaque commemorates her stay at 1 Abbey Terrace. Here is how Gaskell introduces her Whitby:

> a great monastery [Whitby Abbey] had stood on those cliffs, overlooking the vast ocean that blended with the distant sky. Monkshaven itself was built by the side of the Dee, just where the river falls into the German Ocean. The principal street of the town ran parallel to the stream, and smaller lanes branched out of this, and straggled up the sides of the steep hill, between which and the river the houses were pent in. There was a bridge across the Dee, and consequently a Bridge Street running at right angles to the High Street; and on the south side of the stream there were a few houses of more pretension, around which lay gardens and fields. It was on this side of the town that the local aristocracy lived. And who were the great people of this small town? Not the younger branches of the county families that held hereditary state in their manor-houses on the wild bleak moors, that shut in Monkshaven almost as effectually on the land side as ever the waters did on the sea-board. No; these old families kept aloof from the unsavoury yet adventurous trade which brought wealth to generation after generation of certain families in Monkshaven.

> The magnates of Monkshaven were those who had the largest number of ships engaged in the whaling-trade… Every one depended on the whale fishery, and almost every male inhabitant had been, or hoped to be, a sailor. Down by the river the smell was almost intolerable to any

but Monkshaven people during certain seasons of the year; but on these unsavoury 'staithes' the old men and children lounged for hours, almost as if they revelled in the odours of train-oil.

[*Sylvia's Lovers*]

These are Gaskell's moors, Whitby's glorious hinterland:

the country for miles all around was moorland; high above the level of the sea towered the purple crags, whose summits were crowned with greensward that stole down the sides of the scaur a little way in grassy veins. Here and there a brook forced its way from the heights down to the sea, making its channel into a valley more or less broad in long process of time. And in the moorland hollows, as in these valleys, trees and underwood grew and flourished; so that, while on the bare swells of the high land you shivered at the waste desolation of the scenery, when you dropped into these wooded 'bottoms' you were charmed with the nestling shelter which they gave. But above and around these rare and fertile vales there were moors for many a mile, here and there bleak enough, with the red freestone cropping out above the scanty herbage; then, perhaps, there was a brown tract of peat and bog, uncertain footing for the pedestrian who tried to make a short cut to his destination; then on the higher sandy soil there was the purple ling, or commonest species of heather growing in beautiful wild luxuriance.

[*Sylvia's Lovers*]

The Reverend Atkinson would have recognised all of this.

George Gissing (1857–1903)

It is the mind which creates the world around us, and even though we stand side by side in the same meadow, my eyes will never see what is beheld by yours, my heart will never stir to the emotions with which yours is touched.

George Gissing

Author and teacher George Gissing was born and grew up in 2–4 Thompson's Yard, behind 60 Westgate in the Cornmarket area of Wakefield. Many of his twenty-three novels and short stories are informed by his early life in the town. An exhibition in 2017 at the The Gissing Centre, Thompson's Yard, captured this: it took the title of one of George's novels, *A Life's Morning*, which is set in a fictional town with unmistakable echoes of Wakefield. It tells us of the tangled and tortuous love life of a poor but cultured young woman, Emily Hood, from a small town in the north of England in service as a governess to a wealthy country family. This exhibition conjured up a morning walk of 1865 taken by George from his home to the Mechanics' Institute in Wood Street, now Wakefield College's Performing Arts Department. It relates stories behind the buildings he would have passed, some still there, others long gone. George would have seen the frantic preparations for the Wakefield Industrial and Fine Arts Exhibition of 1865, which his father helped to organise.

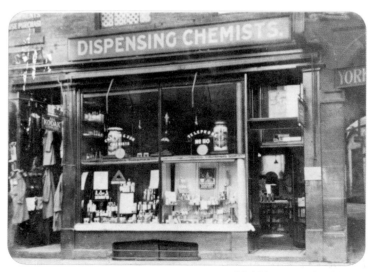

60 Westgate in 1928.

A Life's Morning (1888) narrates the fortunes of a man ruined when his hat blows out of a railway carriage window, leading him down a path of crime; it is clearly set in a version of Wakefield that emerges as Dunfield, with various scenes in Heath Hall, on Heath Common, in Pendal (Sandal) and Banbrigg (Agbrigg).

Banbrigg he describes unflatteringly as follows:

> At no season, and under no advantage of sky, was Banbrigg a delectable abode. Though within easy reach of country which was not without rural aspects, it was marked too unmistakably with the squalor of a manufacturing district... its long, hard ugliness something dispiriting. Though hedges bordered it here and there, they were stunted and grimed; though fields were seen on this side and on that, the grass had absorbed too much mill-smoke to exhibit wholesome verdure...The land was blighted by the curse of what we name – using a word as ugly as the thing it represents – industrialism.

> As the cab brought her along this road from Dunfield station, Emily thought of the downs, the woodlands, the fair pastures of Surrey. There was sorrow at her heart, even a vague tormenting fear. It would be hard to find solace in Banbrigg.

On the face of it, Gissing seems to have despised Wakefield, describing it as 'ingeniously designed for the torment of any man who cares for beauty and tradition' (*Workers in the Dawn* 1880). However, he came back to the town on many occasions to see his sisters Edith and Ellen who ran a school there. This was during a life littered with anguish, disappointment and rejection, failed marriages and imprisonment. In one breath Gissing compares the River Calder to the majestic Tiber in Rome, and then in the next moans about 'mouldering in a Yorkshire village', unable to tolerate Wakefield 'for more than a few days at a time' (*Yorkshire Post*, 16 November 2007). But then, he is forced to admit that he was incapable of being happy anywhere.

For further evidence of his social outlook, his fascination with the working classes, we need go no further than the titles of some of his early books: *Workers in the Dawn* (1880); *The Unclassed* (1884); *Demos* (1886) and the *Nether World* (1889) – all indicators of the urban and political landscape that influenced Gissing as he grew up.

"KINSLEY EVICTIONS"
OCTOBER 3RD 1905

The Kinsley evictions, Wakefield, 1905, when 140 Kinsley miners from the Hemsworth-Fitzwilliam Colliery were served eviction notices when they handed in their notice.

Part of the Humber Bridge at Hessle falls down
shortly before completion in 1981.

John Godber (b. 1956)

There are three routes into Hull – the motorway comes from the west, over the bridge from the south and there's a rail link from Doncaster – and they all end here. Whichever way you look at it, Hull is the end of the line. I suppose geographically Hull is a city on the edge but I like to think Hull is a city on the edge of greatness

John Godber

Born in Hemsworth, a mining community near Pontefract, Godber is the master of the observational comedy and the third most performed English playwright after Shakespeare and Alan Ayckbourn. He trained as a drama teacher at Bretton Hall College in Wakefield, part of the University of Leeds, and became artistic director of Hull Truck Theatre Company in 1984. There he wrote a play directly relevant to his audiences: *Up n' Under* is a production about rugby league in Hull. Many of his other fifty or so plays draw on his Yorkshire roots, including *Bouncers* and *Teechers*. In 2014 a BBC TV programme called *A Picture of Hull* examined John Godber's relationship with Hull where he lives and works, and looked at how it has inspired his work over the last twenty years.

In 2004 he became a visiting professor of Popular Theatre at Liverpool Hope University. In 2005 he won two BAFTAs for *Odd Squad*, written and directed on location in Hull and screened by BBC children's television. He has also spent time as Professor of Drama at Hull University. His *Bouncers* celebrated its 30th anniversary in 2007 and was the final play to be performed by Hull Truck before moving to a new venue – from Spring Street to the new 440-seat theatre in the St Stephen's development. In 2011 he became creative director at Theatre Royal Wakefield and set up The John Godber Company as its resident company.

Of Hull Truck he says

I suppose I came with a mission which was to make theatre viable in traditionally what was a city that perhaps hadn't been able to make theatre work. My mission was to write plays that would attract people who perhaps weren't traditional theatre goers. I wanted to have as wide an audience as possible.

[http://www.bbc.co.uk/humber/content/articles/2005/05/11/
picture_of_britain_john_godber_feature.shtml]

Godber set about transforming the traditional company into a local community theatre, performing plays that reflected ordinary Yorkshire people's lives, from bouncers and teachers to waitresses and coal-board workers. He admits that he has always been inspired by the people and places of Yorkshire and Humberside; his plays have a strong sense of place in that they are immediately identifiable as Yorkshire plays about Yorkshire, making rich use of northern accents and dialect.

In the same interview he tells how

> 'Bouncers' is set in and around a northern nightclub called Mr Cinders, with the action focusing on the exploits of the four doormen and their customers. The play creates a vivid picture of the relentless hedonism of northern night life with its raw energy, flashing disco lights, and raucous lads and lasses out on the town.

> Most people think the play was written about Hull, partly because it has played in the city an amazing 17 times. In fact 'Bouncers' was originally inspired by Kiko's in Pontefract, a Polynesian style night club with fake palm trees. "It's a celebration of the fantastic Bacchanalian aspects of urban night life. Forget 'Look Back in Anger', let's get out there – let's get pissed up," says Godber. As it says in the opening of the play, 'all human life is here' – it's 'a midnight circus'.

The incessant coming and going of ferries to the docks in Hull provides the inspiration for three plays: 'I find it inspiring being on the coast and near the water,' he says. He also is inspired by people-watching in Hull's city centre cafés and Luciano's in Hessle. 'His ability to eaves-drop on conversations from a distance is seen in the witty, crisp dialogue which characterises his plays, and his sharp observations of language and behaviour' [http://www.bbc.co.uk/humber/content/articles/2005/05/11/picture_of_britain_john_godber_feature.shtml].

Spurn Point – the end of the world.

Even though he is often tagged as the voice of Hull, Godber admits 'I've always felt like an outsider, since failing my 11-plus' [http://www.bbc.co.uk/humber/content/articles/2005/05/11/picture_of_britain_john_godber_feature.shtml]. Godber also does much of his thinking outdoors at Spurn Point, another liminal place like Hull, at the end of the line. Being an outsider is a strong theme in Godber's TV drama, *Oddsquad,* shot in Hull using a cast largely drawn from Hull people.

> *Oddsquad* is about a young man, Zack, arriving in Hull with his dad who has just got a new job in the city. It's about coming to terms with being in a new place and how Zack copes with making friends in his new school. John thought that Hull with its 'edge' location was the ideal place to shoot the drama, part of which is set in a caravan on the Humberside coast.
>
> For *Wrestling Mad,* Godber gets his inspiration from Bridlington – the first place where he saw a wrestling match. Godber has eavesdropped on the wrestling scene in Yorkshire, soaking up the atmosphere and snippets of conversations between the sporting protagonists.
>
> [http://www.bbc.co.uk/humber/content/articles/2005/05/11/picture_of_britain_john_godber_feature.shtml]

Street cricket, Victoria Place, Little London, Leeds 1954. © Marc Riboud

Tony Harrison (b. 1937)

Who'd have thought that some of t'most moving poems in t'language would have been composed in a form of English normally reserved for sheep-shaggers and colliers?

Simon Armitage on Tony Harrison

Poet, translator and playwright Tony Harrison was born on Tempest Road, south Leeds, and started his education at Cross Flatts county primary school, Beeston; he later won a scholarship to Leeds Grammar School where he found the tension between his working-class background and the grammar school environment hard to come to terms with; he alludes to this in his poetry, not least in his most anthologised poem, 'Them & [uz]', which recalls the occasion at Leeds Grammar when he was forbidden to recite Keats because of his accent. 'Them & [uz]' asserts 'We'll occupy/your lousy leasehold Poetry', and reveals that in Wordsworth 'matter/water are full rhymes' – thus laying the ground for his ongoing attack on the cultural barriers that divide the classes.

Harrison went on to Leeds University where he studied Classics. His work includes the controversial but critically acclaimed poem 'V' (set at his parents' grave in a Leeds cemetery 'now littered with beer cans and vandalised by obscene graffiti', and *The Trackers of Oxyrhynchus* (1990). There are also fine translations of Aeschylus' *Oresteia* and Aristophanes' L*ysistrata*, Molière's *The Misanthrope*, and *The Mysteries* (1985), an adaptation of the English Medieval Mystery Plays, based on the York and Wakefield cycles. He told Melvyn Bragg in 2012 that 'It was only when I did the *Mystery Plays* and got Northern actors doing verse, that I felt that I was reclaiming the energy of classical verse in the voices that it was created for'. Harrison's 1998 film–poem *Prometheus* has been described as an

> artistic reaction to the fall of the British working class at the end of the twentieth century… the most important adaptation of classical myth for a radical political purpose for years and Harrison's 'most brilliant artwork, with the possible exception of his stage play The Trackers of Oxyrhynchus'.

> [Edith Hall, Tony Harrison's Prometheus:
> A View from the Left]

Harrison's upbringing in working class Leeds with its urban, industrial landscape, had a clear influence on his work. Professor Rick Rylance (Director of the Institute of English Studies, University of London) says that

> his poetry explores themes representative of his generation's experience of increasing social mobility through education that was a feature of post-war life. Typically, this takes the form of meditations on exclusion, like that of Harrison's own family whose origins did not permit much cultural mobility.

> [http://www.poemspoet.com/tony-harrison]

In the poem 'Shrapnel', he links the Blitz of his boyhood to the London bombers of 7 July 2005 who came from the same part of Beeston where he grew up. He recalls 'his mother's metrically ticking knitting needles in a Yorkshire bomb shelter, and indignantly speaking up, in A Cold Coming, for the charred corpse of an Iraqi soldier in the first Gulf war' [*The Guardian*, 31 March 2007].

Mr and Mrs Horace Fawcett relax in their air raid shelter, October 1940 in Cardigan Avenue, Burley – actually a very comfortable reinforced coal cellar; the Leodis website tells that 'the Fawcetts were held up as a shining example of resourcefulness and ingenuity. When members of the ARP came to inspect this shelter, they found the walls neatly papered, electric lighting and a heater installed, chairs and a table, and pictures on the wall, with a cot for the baby in the corner. "It is a grand piece of work" was the comment of Cllr H. W. Sellars, ARP chairman'. Courtesy of Leodis; © Leeds Library & Information Services.

Leeds University likewise had an influence: Harrison rubbed shoulders with many of the Gregory Fellows there, both poets and artists, including Thomas Blackburn, Gregory Fellow in Poetry, and Gregory Fellow in Sculpture Hubert Dalwood whose studio he visited on Cottage Road, Headingley. Harrison valued the importance of contact with 'real artists' that the Gregory Fellowship scheme allowed students. Poet Jon Silkin was another university influence as was James Simmons, with whom he often stayed in his flat on Blenheim Square. Simmons influenced Harrison's own war poetry, written about the First and Second Gulf Wars, and as a 'poet-in-the-field' for *The Guardian* during the war in Bosnia.

Simon Armitage has written in the *New Statesman* how he was 'impressed with the way [Harrison] deals with his upbringing and background in his poems, and more specifically, his accent'. 'Who'd have thought', says Armitage, 'that some of t'most moving poems in t'language would have been composed in a form of English normally reserved for sheep-shaggers and colliers?' [Simon Armitage, 25 April 1997, Tony Harrison is Sixty: Simon Armitage Salutes the Master, p. 45]. To Mary Kaiser in *World Literature Today* Harrison's 'central poetic concern is with a distinctly British problem'. Harrison has a 'predominant fascination with social and class conflict', states Kaiser, who notes that 'throughout his work the dynamic of an overlooked minority resisting an elite and powerful majority plays itself out, whether the context is ancient Greece or Rome, the postwar Leeds of his childhood, or contemporary London'. In Harrison's first major anthology of poetry, *The Loiners* (1970), the author 'explored his relationship with the eponymous citizens of the working-class community of Leeds... from childhood encounters with sex in Leeds...' [*World Literature Today*, winter, 1997, Mary Kaiser, Permanently Bard: Selected Poetry, p. 157].

Leeds city varieties today: 'Music hall was my diet and I think a lot of my work has been a serious metamorphosis of things I saw as a child.'

Another important local influence on Harrison's work were the variety shows he watched as a boy in Leeds. Of this he says:

> Music hall was my diet and I think a lot of my work has been a serious metamorphosis of things I saw as a child. It was quite hard to think about verse drama when I started out. It was Eliot and Fry, which I didn't like. I thought they ruined verse drama. But the verse of musicals and of pantomime was wonderful. I remember men playing women and women playing men speaking in verse, and I think those experiences go quite deep.

> [Nicholas Wroe, *The Guardian*, 1 April 2000]

Hepworth drawing on Rosewall, near St Ives, 1961

Barbara Hepworth (1903–1975)

Whenever I am embraced by land and seascape I draw ideas for new sculptures: new forms to touch and walk round, new people to embrace, with an exactitude of form that those without sight can hold and realize.

Barbara Hepworth, from *Barbara Hepworth: Drawings from a Sculptor's Landscape*, 1966

Barbara Hepworth has written extensively on the importance of and the role landscapes play in her work. To illustrate this as clearly as possible and to show how perhaps similar experiences may have inspired or at least influenced other writers in this book, I make no excuse for quoting at length from her writings.

Hepworth was born in Wakefield into an upwardly mobile family: her father encouraged her to get on in life. Significantly, as a child she accompanied her father, Herbert, when he travelled all over the West Yorkshire countryside with his job as a civil engineer for the West Riding County Council, and, from 1921, County Surveyor. Hepworth attended Wakefield Girls' High School and won a music scholarship in 1915 and an Open Scholarship in 1917. Summer holidays, significantly again, were spent at beautiful Robin Hood's Bay. These were not the usual bucket and spade and donkey ride affairs; Hepworth's beach holidays were not without influence and came back to delight her later in life:

> My father took us each year to Robin Hood's Bay to stay in a house on the lovely beach... here I laid out my paints and general paraphernalia and crept out at dawn to collect stones, seaweeds and paint, and draw by myself before somebody organised me!

> [*Barbara Hepworth, A Pictorial Autobiography*, 1971]

Hepworth at Robin Hood's Bay, 1925

In 1920–1921 she was a student at Leeds School of Art where she met Henry Moore, a fellow student, friend and friendly rival. She then won a county scholarship to the Royal College of Art where she studied from 1921 and was awarded the diploma of the Royal College of Art in 1924.

One early instance of Hepworth's relationship with landscape came in 1953 where the film *Figures in a Landscape: Cornwall and the Sculpture of Barbara Hepworth* made by Dudley Shaw Ashton for the British Film Institute was shown. In 1966 Alan Bowness', *Barbara Hepworth: Drawings from a Sculptor's Landscape* was published; 2003 saw the publication of *Barbara Hepworth and the Yorkshire Landscape: An Anthology of her Writings and Recollections*, by Sophie Bowness.

In *Drawings from a Sculptor's Landscape* we can see how those early car journeys must have created an impact and left an indelible impression: she describes how all living things form part of her creative landscape:

> A sculptor's landscape embraces all things that grow and live and are articulate in principle: the shape of the buds already formed in autumn, the thrust and fury of spring growth, the adjustment of trees and rocks and human beings to the fierceness of winter – all these belong to the sculptor's world, as well as the supreme perception of man, woman and child of this expanding universe.

She fully explains that impact in *Extracts from Barbara Hepworth, A Pictorial Autobiography*, (Bath, 1971) in existential terms: *she is the landscape*:

> All my early memories are of forms and shapes and textures. Moving through and over the West Riding landscape with my father in his car, the hills were sculptures; the roads defined the form. Above all, there was the sensation of moving physically over the contours of fulnesses and concavities, through hollows and over peaks – feeling, touching, seeing, through mind and hand and eye. This sensation has never left me. I, the sculptor, *am* the landscape. I am the form and I am the hollow, the thrust and the contour.

And:

> For a few years I became the object. I was the figure in the landscape and every sculpture contained to a greater or lesser degree the ever-changing forms and contours embodying my own response to a given position in that landscape. [...] There is no landscape without the human figure: it is impossible for me to contemplate pre-history in the abstract. Without the relationship of man and his land the mental image becomes a nightmare.

> I used colour and strings in many of the carvings of this time. The colour in the concavities plunged me into the depth of water, caves, or shadows deeper than the carved concavities themselves. The strings were the tension I felt between myself and the sea, the wind or the hills. The barbaric and magical countryside of rocky hills, fertile valleys, and dynamic coastline of West Penwith has provided me with a background and a soil which compare in strength with those of my childhood in the West Riding. Moreover it has supplied me with one of my greatest needs

for carving: a strong sunlight and a radiance from the sea which almost surrounds this spit of land, as well as a milder climate which enables me to carve out of doors nearly the whole year round.

[Barbara Hepworth, *The War, Cornwall, and Artist in Landscape, 1939–1946*, Chapter 4]

Rocks above Ilkley from a selection of photographs commissioned by Hepworth in 1964 for *Drawings for a Sculptor's Landscape*. All three courtesy of Sophie Bowness, Hepworth Estate.

Dales lambscape above Litton.

James Herriot (1916–1995)

loosely autobiographical books about life as a vet in the Yorkshire Dales in the 1930s and 1940s...Herriot's books are not only funny, they contain just about everything that is good in life: the English countryside, silly animals, and love. Joyful stuff.

The Times, 9 September 2017

James Herriot is the pen name for James Alfred 'Alf' Wight, a veterinary surgeon who tapped into his experiences as a vet in the Yorkshire Dales west and north of Thirsk to produce a series of semi-autobiographical works, beginning with *If Only They Could Talk* in 1970. The highly popular television series based on the books was called *All Creatures Great and Small*.

The landscape above Hawes.

The Dales landscapes are inextricably bound up in these stories – all the more obvious from the visual impressions afforded by the television series. Herriot was born in Sunderland and came to Thirsk after a spell in Glasgow where he qualified as a vet in 1939, and some time in a practice back in Sunderland. In Thirsk the rural practice was at 23 Kirkgate in Skeldale House. The name 'James Herriot' was adopted after he watched Scottish goalkeeper Jim Herriot play for Birmingham City against Manchester United on the TV.

Herriot's stories – half autobiographical half fiction – describe a rural practice operating at a time of great change for veterinary medicine in the UK: draught horses were increasingly replaced by tractors; farm machinery was supplementing farm labour; small animal medicine was on the increase and antibiotics were wiping out some disease and ancient folk remedies. The books describe such delights as a hysterectomy on a cat and a Caesarean section on a cow.

In the books, Herriot lives and works in Darrowby, a composite of Thirsk, Richmond, Leyburn and Middleham, although much of the filming for Darrowby scenes was done in Askrigg, in Wensleydale; pub scenes for the Drover's Arms were shot in Askrigg's old King's Arms.

Scarborough Bay from the castle

Susan Hill (b. 1942)

Memory is like a long, dark street, illuminated at intervals in a light so bright that it shows up every detail. And then one plunges into the dark stretch again.

Susan Hill, *Howards End Is on the Landing: A Year of Reading from Home*

Susan Hill is a prolific author of fiction and non-fiction books. She was born in Scarborough and from the age of three attended Scarborough Convent School where she developed an interest in the theatre and literature before relocating with her family in 1958 to Coventry. While in Scarborough, Hill, from a young age, attended many performances at the Scarborough Repertory Theatre, which was twinned with the Repertory in York, and alternated productions. When the Stephen Joseph Theatre in the Round opened in a large room above the Scarborough Library she went there as often as possible too.

The castle around 1900

She describes Scarborough as

> a beautiful place, with dramatic cliffs, two sweeping bays, amazing views, a Castle, a Harbour with fishing boats.... And when I was growing up there, it was a very genteel resort, full of retired and older people. Of course there were young people and I had plenty of school friends, but I still remember it as a place full of the old.

[www.susan-hill.com/pages/about_susan/biography.asp]

This memory of 'oldness' may have something to do with the 'days gone by' aura that pervades some of her work, such as *The Various Haunts of Men* (2004) set in a cocooned cathedral town.

Hill refers to Scarborough and the 'oldness' of Scarborough life in her novel *A Change for the Better* (1969) – the blurb for which describes how 'In the Prince of Wales Hotel and the shabby terraces and tearooms of Westbourne, retired lives run their course – all, in their different ways, anticipating crisis' and in short stories such as *A Bit of Singing and Dancing* and particularly in *Cockles and Mussels*. Here the fascination with Scarborough's characteristic 'oldness' finds Miss Avis Parson staying at Mrs Muriel Hennessy's guest house, populated with mainly elderly guests. The Lower Bay, a haunt of undesirables, is visible from the guest house's window: one night Avis decides to explore this no-go area where all that is dangerous to her hitherto cautious and tidy life seems to thrive:

> The story uses a subtle use of symbolism in the cockles and mussels that Avis eats during her night out, the gritty taste of them seems to represent all that she has kept distant from her life, things people have perhaps told her not to become involved with, the unlived aspect of her life, a chance meeting with Mrs Rourke, the guest house cook, though has big consequences for the two women.

[theendlessbeginning.wordpress.com/tag/susan-hill/]

In *The Conservatory* she writes about Wood End, the Scarborough marine villa in which the Sitwell family grew up: Osbert, Edith and Sacheverell Sitwell made a significant impression on Hill; it is now an Arts and Crafts Gallery. More about Hill's life in Scarborough can be found in *Family* (1989).

Sheffield Road, Hoyland Common.

Barry Hines (1939–2016)

I wasn't only captivated by the characters and the plot, though. What really made me grin and bang the settee arm...was the way the characters spoke: they talked just like me. Somehow Hines...managed to get that minimalist Barnsley poetry down on the page without the apostrophes flying round the paragraphs like racing pigeons... Yorkshire found its voice in Kes.

Ian McMillan on first looking into a copy of
A Kestrel for a Knave

Barry Hines was born in the mining village of Hoyland Common near Barnsley; he went to Ecclesfield Grammar School and played football for the England Grammar Schools team. Five O Levels later he took a job with the National Coal Board as an apprentice mining surveyor at Rockingham Colliery, Tankersley, Barnsley, but decided to return to school when a neighbour saw him at the coalface and acidly asked 'Couldn't tha find a better job than this?' He got four A Levels and then studied for a PE teaching qualification at prestigious Loughborough College. After this he was a Physical Education teacher for several years, first in a London comprehensive and then at Longcar Central School in Barnsley, where he studiously wrote novels in the library after the children had gone home. He later became a full-time writer.

Hines, of course, is best known for his 1968 novel *A Kestrel for a Knave*; he also wrote the script for the film, *Kes*, directed by Ken Loach. The influence of his upbringing in Barnsley and its industrial landscape are tangible: the book tells the story of a schoolboy, the emblem of a ragged generation, Billy Casper. Billy was afflicted with what we now call 'issues'; he came from a mining village near Barnsley and finds solace in adopting and looking after a kestrel that he names 'Kes'. Hines also wrote the script for the BAFTA award-winning TV film *Threads* (1984), a disturbing television drama on the effects of nuclear war on Sheffield.

This is how Hines remembered his junior school in 1999 – themes and images immediately reflected and detectable in *A Kestrel for a Knave*:

> The rooms were dark, the furniture was old and the teachers seemed old – even if they weren't: some of them were in their twenties or thirties but they had the clothes and haircuts of their dads. Mr Blackledge, the headmaster, had some fingers blown off during the war, and your eyes were always drawn to his hand. For corporal punishment, he would crouch down and his hand would go behind your bare legs (we wore short trousers) – and the thought of the gammy hand at the back of my legs, like something out of a horror film, was worse than the actual punishment. The absolute pit: Our junior school seemed to get more people through the 'scholarship' to grammar school than other nearby primary schools. Mr Blackledge used to choose about 15 children: those of us considered to have a chance of getting through. These special lessons were a double streaming: a dozen or so taken out and the rest of even the 'A' stream abandoned. The boys who didn't pass went to the very rough secondary

modern up the road, just passing the time until they went at 15 down the mine or to the steelworks.

[www.independent.co.uk/news/people/profiles/education-passedfailed-barry-hines-1085784.html]

Hines is well known for writing scripts in Yorkshire dialect. Ken Loach said of this, 'He loved language and his ear for the dialect and its comedy was pitch perfect' [*The Guardian*, 23 March 2016]. The use of dialect is especially prominent, as is Hines's deployment of his industrial landscape, in *Kes* and in *The Price of Coal* (1977) – a two-part television drama written by Barry Hines and directed by Ken Loach. It is set at the fictional Milton Colliery, near Barnsley in South Yorkshire and contrasts 'efforts made to cosmetically improve the pit in preparation for a royal visit and the target-conscious safety shortcuts that precipitate a fatal accident' [Keith Bruce, *The Herald*, 11 Jun 2005]. The drama draws on the Cadeby Main Pit Disaster on 9 July 1912 at Cadeby Main Colliery, near Doncaster, killing 91 men while the King and Queen were visiting pit villages in Yorkshire. Characters use Yorkshire dialect almost throughout; both episodes were shown with subtitles. The drama was filmed on location at the disused Thorpe Hesley colliery near Rotherham while the scenes involving the ill-fated Mines Rescue Team were shot in Wakefield with the real Mines Rescue Team.

HOYLAND SILKSTONE COLLIERY

Hoyland Silkstone Colliery – typical of the industrial landscape.

A Kestrel for a Knave, though, was by no means the only work to emerge from Hines's south Yorkshire hinterland. *The Gamekeeper* (1975) is a powerful portrayal of the way stately homes and landowners have shaped the north; as Hines put it, both book and film 'were about class, not gamekeepers. You don't have to say anything; you just show it' [http://www.screenonline.org.uk/tv/id/557164/index.html]; and *Looks and Smiles* (1981) expatiates on how the first wave of redundancies and closures dealt a body blow to the steelworks in Sheffield in the late 1970s and early 1980s.

The Guardian's obituary for Hines read, 'In "The Price of Coal" he revealed not only his angry compassion for the daily dangers of mining, but an acknowledgment of the feudal backwardness in his community' [20 March 2016].

Leeds, May 1955

Richard Hoggart (1918–2014)

'Who are the working classes?', which occupies the opening section of [The Uses of Literacy]. It blends scraps of literature, popular song, cheap journalism, personal observation and scenes from Hoggart's own early provincial life into an almost psychological investigation.

D. J. Taylor in *The Guardian*, 24 February 2007

The impoverished Potternewton area of Leeds is where Richard Hoggart grew up, one of three children in a very poor family. His soldier father was a housepainter and veteran of both the Boer War and the Great War, who died of brucellosis when Hoggart was one year old; his mother died when he was eight. He later spoke movingly and poignantly about his family's abject poverty:

> When I see – or see film of – a driven bird flying to its nest and anxiously, earnestly feeding the open mouths, the image of our mother comes to mind…When you have seen a woman standing frozen, while tears start slowly down her cheeks because a sixpence has been lost … you do not easily forget.

Such experience was to inform Hoggart's work. Following his mother's death the eight-year-old Hoggart was then raised by a loving widowed grandmother in Hunslet, in a typically overcrowded cottage, its one claim to fame being that it was the only mains-connected cottage in the street. The perceptive and indomitable Aunt Ethel, a tailor, lived there too: she focussed on young Richard when a head teacher picked him out as a pupil with promise. Ethel quickly realised that this might be Richard's chance to escape the shackles restricting him to his class. She urged him to concentrate on his education, the result of which saw him follow big brother, Tom, to Cockburn High School, a grammar school, assisted by hardship grants from the Board of Guardians and the Royal British Legion. He failed the 11-plus maths paper, but won a scholarship thanks to his English essay, supported by a plea from his junior school head teacher to re-mark his paper. Hoggart later discovered that his coveted scholarship was one of only thirty available at the time for a catchment of 65,000 children of his age. This 'close-thing' experience inculcated a lifelong support for comprehensive education.

Hoggart also never forgot the gratitude he owed to his extended family for inspiring him; he never forgot how fortunate he was to win that rare scholarship. Putting his earlier maths failure behind him, he gained the equivalent of a distinction in O level maths. He then won a scholarship to study English at the University of Leeds in 1936, from which he graduated with a First. Again, sheer hard work was the key to his success: his was one of a mere forty-seven Leeds University scholarships available to his class of 8,000 18-year-olds. In his obituary of Hoggart [*The Guardian*, Thursday 10 April 2014] John Ezard wrote: 'While Cockburn grammar school eventually took the boy out of Hunslet, he never let it take Hunslet out of the boy.'

How the Luftwaffe neatly converted this semi into a detached house on 22 September 1941 in a cul-de-sac off Cliff Road. Courtesy of Leodis; © Leeds Library & Information Services.

From 1946 to 1959 Hoggart held a post as an extramural tutor at the University of Hull where he published his first book, a comprehensive study of W. H. Auden's poetry, in 1951. The book for which he is most famous, the classic *The Uses of Literacy: Aspects of Working Class Life*, was published in 1957. It is partly autobiographical, drawing on his youthful experience of working class life and has been seen as a detailed first-hand account of the loss of Britain's authentic working class popular culture, deploring the tidal wave of a mass culture through post-war advertising, the influences of mass-media and Americanisation which arrived in the mid to late forties. These modish concepts, Hoggart observed, were to change British urban working-class people forever – their lives, their urban landscape, values and culture.

Betting shop in the Turk's Head Yard, of Briggate 1954. © Marc Riboud

His lifelong belief in the value of education – thanks in no small part to that visionary Aunt Ethel – saw him working on numerous cultural quangos and causes including public libraries, adult education and the arts. This culminated in his post as Arts Council vice-chairman, until, that is, Margaret Thatcher (characteristically showing none of Aunt Ethel's vision) sacked him in 1982. Prolific and workaholic to the extreme, the insecurities fostered by his early life made him nervous of ever going freelance; he himself mused whether his readiness to serve on committees (not being able to say no, in effect) was a result of a childhood that had left him 'unusually glad to find myself wanted'.

Of course, *The Uses of Literacy* was just one of many works produced by Richard Hoggart. It is probably safe to assume that most if not all were influenced by the urban landscape and its people, which Hoggart met every day in Potternewton and Hunslet.

Interestingly, one of his later works was *Townscape with Figures: Farnham, Portrait of a Town* (1994) written in retirement.

Scarborough.

Winifred Holtby (1898–1935)

*She is the daughter of a Yorkshire farmer and learnt to read
… while minding the pigs – hence her passion for me.*

Virginia Wolf on Winifred Holtby

Winifred Holtby, feminist, socialist and pacifist, journalist and novelist, was born in Long Street, Rudston, a Wolds village between Driffield and Bridlington. Her parents once lived in a house in Cottingham, just north of Hull, which was later renamed Holtby House, owned by the university; Philip Larkin lived there when he first arrived in Hull in 1955. Holtby was first educated at home, then at Queen Margaret's School, Scarborough, where she passed the entrance exam for Somerville College, Oxford, in 1917; she chose to join the Women's Army Auxiliary Corps (WAAC) in early 1918 instead but on arriving in France, the First World War ended and she returned home. In 1919 she finally went up to Oxford where she met Vera Brittain, with whom she was friends for the rest of her life. After graduating in 1921, the pair moved to London with a view to becoming writers, as attested by the blue plaque at 52 Doughty Street, their rented flat in Bloomsbury.

While a boarder at Queen Margaret's School in Scarborough, she witnessed the bombardment of the town by the German fleet in December 1914. Her recollections were later published in a Cumberland newspaper. The bombardment recurs in her novel *The Crowded Street* (1924). From her earliest novels, the landscapes of Holtby's Yorkshire Wolds are clearly visible. Her first, 1923's *Anderby Wold*, is the story of Mary Robson, a young Yorkshire woman, married to her dull cousin John with whom she battles to maintain Mary's ramshackle inheritance, Anderby Wold, in an agricultural community beset by massive social change – socialism and the unionisation of rural labour. Mary is wearied by her struggle and by the innate stubbornness of the traditional Yorkshire conservatism she encounters. The arrival of sophisticated and eloquent David Rossitur, a young man from a different England, radical and devoted to social change, challenges and changes Mary and the sleepy village of Anderby forever.

Scarborough shell damage after the 1914 bombardment. The shop is a grocer's in Prospect Street – the owner's wife was killed in the doorway while helping casualties. Whitby and the Hartlepools were also shelled on the same day.

Here, then, we have another example of a bright Yorkshire person anxious to exchange their uneventful Yorkshire lives for something a lot more exciting. Holtby would, of course, have empathised with her hero when she herself escaped Rudston.

The Yorkshire landscape also features in *The Crowded Street* (1924). There's social suffocation here, too, and restrictions imposed on opportunities for women. *The Crowded Street* introduces us to twenty-year-old Muriel Hammond, cocooned in the confines of stifling Edwardian middle-class society in Marshington, a Yorkshire village. No career is permitted to her. Muriel is shy, unconfident and prey to the small town expectations; marriage is proving a particular challenge. The First World War gives Muriel the chance she, and her sister, need to break out and take advantage of the work, friendship, freedom the war offers, exchanging her enforced idleness with 'an idea of service – not just vague and sentimental, but translated into quite practical things' [*The Crowded Street*, p. 270].

The Land Of Green Ginger (1927) is a reference to that wonderfully named street in Hull spotted as a child by the novel's hero, Joanna Burton, who is born in South Africa but packed off back to England by her missionary father to be brought up in Yorkshire. Later, when her husband returns wounded from the First World War, Joanna faces the harsh reality of motherhood and life on a Yorkshire farm. It recalls the Dales, where Holtby's mother was born.

Holtby's finest work is the never-out-of-print *South Riding*, edited by Vera Brittain and published posthumously in March 1936; in 1974 it was adapted by Stan Barstow for Yorkshire Television. Vera Brittain wrote about her friendship with Holtby in *Testament of Friendship* (1940). Their letters, along with many of Holtby's other papers, are now held at the Hull History Centre. Other papers are deposited in Bridlington library.

South Riding takes us back to Holtby's own Yorkshire with a moving portrait of a rural community struggling with the effects of the Depression, a panorama of the author's Yorkshire and its people. Brittain was Holtby's executor and immediately faced opposition to the publication of the book in the shape of Holtby's indomitable mother, Alice, the first woman alderman of the East Riding. She was fearful lest her daughter's depiction of the mundanities and minutiae of local government, based on what she had told her, might expose her to criticism and ridicule. Holtby junior insisted that she had used sources 'unknown to you', although we know that she rummaged through her mother's litter bin and salvaged screwed up council minutes – what Shirley Williams calls 'an early example of investigative journalism'. The book was published and Alice Holtby immediately resigned.

Shirley Williams, Vera Brittain's daughter and Holtby's adopted niece, confirms the inspiration for the book:

> Winifred Holtby's masterpiece, was born of two powerful factors in her life: her deep roots in the Yorkshire countryside and her fascination with the comedies and tragedies of local government. The first was nourished by accompanying her father, David Holtby, around his Rudston farm in the wolds of the East Riding, a land of rich earth and huge skies. The second began with admiration for her mother, the formidable Alice Holtby.

> [*The Independent*, 19 February 2011]

Holtby's Yorkshire is all over *South Riding* – a fictional place and a complement to the real worlds of the North, West and East Ridings. For South Riding, read East Riding, the location of Rudston. Kingsport is Kingston-upon-Hull; Flintonbridge is Beverley; Kiplington, the coastal town where Sarah Burton is headmistress, is a conflation of Hornsea and Withernsea, the towns where Holtby took lodgings while writing the book. Cold Harbour Colony, the ex-servicemen's colony of smallholdings, is Sunk Island in Holderness; Robert Carne's decaying Maythorpe Hall gets its inspiration from White Hall in Winestead. At Withernsea in 1934, she interrupted her writing to hand out anti-fascist leaflets outside a meeting of Yorkshire Blackshirts.

The book champions and challenges, through the hero, Sarah Burton, a raft of contemporary social issues, including education, unemployment, local building programmes, poor relief and the treatment of the mentally ill. Sarah is a progressive head teacher at the local school; other key characters are local impoverished farmer Robert Carne, and local alderman Emma Beddows who is modelled on the author's mother.

South Riding fused her deep feeling for the wolds countryside of her youth with her progressive politics, to create a harmonious picture of provincial life in the area surrounding Hull.

[Susanna Rustin, *The Guardian*, 14 January 201]

Holtby rushed *South Riding* to a conclusion in the knowledge that she was dying from Bright's disease (nephritis); it is no surprise then that death and disease pervade the book: Joe Astell has got tuberculosis, Lily Sawdon, the publican's wife, is dying from cancer, Mrs Holly dies in childbirth, Carne suffers from heart disease. Conversely, the novel's closing lines has 'a serene old age' waiting for Mrs Beddows, a fate denied Holtby who endured a decidedly bleak personal landscape for the two years following her diagnosis.

Shirley Williams adds another, less well known, dimension to Holtby's innate compassion – a quality that shines out from the book and its characters:

> Yet her generous spirit was unable to refuse help to her friends, to the poor, the homeless and the desperate. In the last few months of her life, as she fought to complete South Riding, she also cared for her sick niece Anne, for her mother, and for my brother John and me when my mother, Winifred's dearest friend, was coping with my father's serious illness and her own father's suicide.

[*Independent*, 19 February 2011]

As Mark Bostridge concludes [in his *Guardian* review of Andrew Davies' BBC adaptation, 19 February 2011]:

> Sarah is Holtby herself, never more so than when she is defending the right of single women to lead fruitful, independent lives. 'I was born to be a spinster,' Sarah tells herself, 'and by God, I'm going to spin'. Burton puts her trust in the power of collective action by local government to create a more beneficent 'English landscape'.

Here Holtby is using her Yorkshire literary landscape to achieve a better social landscape for England.

Ted Hughes (1930–1998)

What's writing really about? It's about trying to take fuller possession of the reality of your life.

Ted Hughes

Ted Hughes was born at 1 Aspinall Street, in Mytholmroyd which is near Hebden Bridge, between Burnley and Halifax. His early life was spent among the farms of the Calder Valley and on the Pennines above Mytholmroyd. Hughes himself says that 'my first six years shaped everything' [*The Daily Telegraph*, 2 November 1998]. So, we can take it that the rural landscape by which he was surrounded was destined to exert a significant influence on his later work as a poet and writer.

Mytholmroyd

In 1938 the family moved to Mexborough near Doncaster where they ran a tobacconists and newsagents. It was here that Hughes says, in *Poetry in Making*, that he cultivated his fascination for animals, making lead models of them; he acted as retriever for his gamekeeper elder brother gathering shot magpies, owls, rats and curlews around the farms in the valleys and on the moors. Manor

Farm at Old Denaby, was a favourite, which he said he would come to know 'better than any place on earth'. His earliest poem 'The Thought Fox', and first story 'The Rain Horse' recall this. Hughes learnt much about wildlife from his close friend John Wholly's father, a gamekeeper; 'fishing became almost a religious experience' [Keith Sagar, *Ted Hughes, Fishing and Poetry*].

In 1951, after National Service at RAF Patrington in east Yorkshire, Hughes went up to Pembroke College, Cambridge. At desolate Patrington, Hughes had little else to do but 'read and reread Shakespeare and watch the grass grow' [*Guardian*, 14 January 2011], learning many of the plays off by heart; Yeats got the same treatment. In 1952 the family went back to West Yorkshire to live at The Beacon, Heptonstall, not far from Hebden Bridge.

Hughes's exposure to the farms and moorlands around his homes certainly influenced his poetry: this rural landscape and the animals that populated it (domestic and wild) re-emerge in his earlier poetic work where nature is ubiquitous, particularly the paradox of the beauty and violence that co-exist. Animals such as the hawk, horse and jaguar are emblems of Hughes's poetic world. The Poetry Foundation puts it well:

> The rural landscape of Hughes's youth in Yorkshire exerted a lasting influence on his work. To read Hughes's poetry is to enter a world dominated by nature, especially by animals. This holds true for nearly all of his books, from The Hawk in the Rain to Wolfwatching (1989) and Moortown Diary (1989), two of his late collections. Hughes's love of animals was one of the catalysts in his decision to become a poet. According to London Times contributor Thomas Nye, Hughes once confessed 'that he began writing poems in adolescence, when it dawned upon him that his earlier passion for hunting animals in his native Yorkshire ended either in the possession of a dead animal, or at best a trapped one. He wanted to capture not just live animals, but the aliveness of animals in their natural state: their wildness, their quiddity, the fox-ness of the fox and the crow-ness of the crow.'

[www.poetryfoundation.org/poets/ted-hughes]

But it is in *The Remains of Elmet* (1979) a threnody in which Hughes explores and laments the vanishing landscapes of his younger days most explicitly; the British Library entry puts it best:

> The work responds to the landscape and people of the Calder valley, the place of Hughes's birth and early childhood. Hughes expands on his subject in the Preface to the 1979 edition:
>
> The Calder valley, west of Halifax, was the last ditch of Elmet, the last British Celtic kingdom to fall to the Angles. For centuries it was considered a more or less uninhabitable wilderness, a notorious refuge for criminals, a hide-out for refugees. Then in the early 1800s it became the cradle for the Industrial Revolution in textiles, and the upper Calder became 'the hardest-worked river in England'. Throughout my lifetime, since 1930, I have watched the mills of the region and their attendant chapels die. Within the last fifteen years the end has come. They are now virtually dead, and the population of the valley and the hillsides, so rooted for so long, is changing rapidly.
>
> Hughes's 'pennine sequence', as he titled it, presents a poetic vision of the valley that evokes the myths, histories and collective memories weaved into this unyielding land and its people. His taut verse and Godwin's evocative photography do not merely describe but also embody the rhythms, sounds and atmosphere of the area.
>
> [bl.uk/collection-items/remains-of-elmet-by-ted-hughes-with-photographs-by-fay-godwin]

The British Library goes on to add that

> The Preface and the 'Remains' of the title signal that this is a lament for what has been lost, yet the sequence also reads as an affirmation of the transcendent power contained within the landscape. Hughes held this belief in common with Emily Brontë, who had also lived in West Yorkshire. As Hughes writes in the Preface, the land holds a 'spectacular desolation', a 'grim sort of beauty'.

These words are from the Library's description of their first edition, presentation copy of *The Remains of Elmet* inscribed by Hughes. The inscription includes two stanzas of unpublished verse comparing Heptonstall and Halifax.

St Mary's Church – the view from the church door.

Margaret Storm Jameson (1891–1986)

Language is memory and metaphor.

Storm Jameson

Storm Jameson was born in Whitby into a family that can trace its Whitby roots back some 600 years. Her father was a sea captain, and her mother was from an old-established local family shipping firm.

Storm Jameson grew up at 5 Park Terrace, North Bank, before moving to West Cliff. She went to Scarborough Municipal School and won one of the three North Riding scholarships to Leeds University where she gained a First in English Literature and Language.

A one-year research scholarship to University College, London, and a spell at King's College followed where she delivered an MA on modern drama. At this time, women undergraduates were still a rare thing; postgraduates rarer still. Storm Jameson was a socialist and a suffragist at this point in her life. Later, she worked as a teacher and as a copywriter with an advertising agency before taking up writing full time.

Her first marriage dissolved, she met and married Guy Chapman, a professor of modern history at Leeds University, in 1926.

Whitby features large in her autobiography *Journey From the North* (1969). Volume One tells of her childhood in Whitby before the First World War, the strong relationship she enjoyed with her mother, her love of the sea and her academic achievements at university.

In all, she wrote forty-seven novels, as well as essays, short stories and criticism – between 1919 and 1979. Her work, though, and her life, is shared between active politics, feminism and pacifism and her 'Whitby' novels. From 1938 to 1945, she was president of PEN (Poets, Essayists, Novelists), in which she assisted refugee writers from her own pocket and with funds contributed by other English writers. During the war, she was chairman of the Society of Authors.

The burial ground at St Mary's Church.

Much of her work is autobiographical, at least in part: the landscapes and seascapes she saw all around her are clearly evident. Whitby gave her the model for Danesacre, a town that crops up in several of her books. It's there in *None Turn Back* and *The Road from the Monument*. Whitby (Danesacre) is Wik in *The Moon is Making*. Storm Jameson came back to Whitby frequently to visit her family, and also lived for a time at nearby Ruswarp. She wrote *A Day Off* (1933) in a moorland house near to Whitby in which she had lived since 1929.

The Triumph of Time trilogy (based on her own family history): *The Lovely Ship* (1927), *The Voyage Home* (1930) and *A Richer Dust* (1931) are full of descriptions of Whitby while the Mary Hervey Russell books – *Company Parade* (1934); *The Mirror in Darkness I* and II; Love in Winter (1935); None Turn Back (1936) The Mirror in Darkness III; The Journal of Mary Hervey Russell (1945); Before the Crossing (1947); and The Black Laurel (1947) all tell the story of Mary Hansyke, later Mary Hervey, from her birth in 1841 to her death in 1923. Mary is based on the life of her own grandmother who came from a long line of shipbuilders and who took over the running of the business herself. In 1932 Storm Jameson, like Winifred Holtby, became close friends with Vera Brittain.

In Company Parade (1934), Storm Jameson describes how one of the characters, Russell Harvey, and her mother attend the 1921 Armistice Day service at St Mary's Church, and describes the view from the church door overlooking the harbour, the hills around it and the sea. The book ends with the main character looking down on Danesacre from the road above the town. She wants to love Danesacre but she can't – she wants to go back to London…

Geoffrey Anketell Studdert Kennedy, MC aka 'Woodbine Willie' (1883–1929)

Waste of Blood, and waste of Tears, Waste of youth's most precious years, Waste of ways the saints have trod, Waste of Glory, waste of God, War!

'Waste', *More Rough Rhymes of a Padre*, 1919

Kennedy was an English Anglican priest and poet. He is best remembered by his nickname 'Woodbine Willie', earned during the war for lavishing Woodbine cigarettes along with spiritual aid on injured and dying soldiers with no regard for his own safety.

He was born in Leeds, the seventh of nine children born to Jeanette Anketell and William Studdert Kennedy, vicar of St Mary's, in the impoverished Quarry Hill area. In 1914 Leeds, then the fifth largest city in England, had 78,000 back-to-backs; back-to-back housing construction had been made illegal in 1909 but a loophole in the law meant that new back-to-backs were still being built in Leeds up to the 1930s.

Studdert Kennedy was educated at Leeds Grammar School and Trinity College, Dublin, where he graduated in Classics and Divinity in 1904. He then trained at Ripon Clergy College before going on to posts in Rugby and Worcester.

Apparently, his charismatic way converted more men over a pint of beer than most vicars could achieve in their churches in a lifetime. At the outbreak of war Studdert Kennedy volunteered as a chaplain to the army on the Western Front; in 1917 he was awarded the Military Cross at Messines Ridge in Flanders after he dashed into no man's land to fetch morphine and tend the wounded during an attack on the German frontline. His citation read:

For conspicuous gallantry and devotion to duty. He showed the greatest courage and disregard for his own safety in attending to the wounded under heavy fire. He searched shell holes for our own and enemy wounded, assisting them to the dressing station, and his cheerfulness and endurance had a splendid effect upon all ranks in the front line trenches, which he constantly visited.

['No. 30234', *The London Gazette (Supplement)*, 14 August 1917, p. 8384]

To Studdert Kennedy, ministry simply meant taking 'a box of fags in your haversack, and a great deal of love in your heart' and he said 'you can pray with them sometimes; but pray for them always' [Bob Holman, *Woodbine Willie: An Unsung Hero of World War One*, 2013, p. 165]. Ironically, he was a heavy smoker, despite also being asthmatic and having suffered the effects of mustard gas.

One story has him in the thick of intense fighting crawling out to a working party putting up wire in front of their trench. A soldier asked him who he was, to which he replied 'The Church'. When the soldier asked what the Church was doing out there, he replied 'Its job'.

A published poet, he authored *Rough Rhymes of a Padre* (1918), and *More Rough Rhymes* (1919). During the Great War he was an enthusiastic promoter of the British war machine: attached to a bayonet-training unit, he toured with boxers and wrestlers to give morale-boosting speeches and demonstrations about the usefulness and efficacy of the bayonet. However, his Damascene moment came when he stopped talking to, and started listening to, the soldiers, spreading their views on ending the war, their distaste for the monarchy, and their hopes for the end of poverty back home. His poems, many of which are written in working-class Yorkshire dialect, project their views in their own words and language. Nevertheless, he apparently believed that in principle it was better for young men to be challenged by facing German guns than resorting to prostitutes and so established self-help groups for men tempted by prostitutes and drink.

His father's work in Quarry Hill and his experience of the ingrained poverty there in its unremittingly bleak urban landscape must surely have influenced and affected Studdert Kennedy and his work, both literary and pastoral. Post war, Studdert Kennedy, was critical of the war; he converted to Christian socialism; he wrote *Lies* (1919); *Democracy and the Dog-Collar* (1921) with intentionally inflammatory chapter headings such as 'The Church Is Not a Movement but a Mob', 'Capitalism is Nothing But Greed, Grab, and Profit-Mongering' and 'So-Called Religious Education Worse than Useless'; *Food for the Fed Up* (1921), *The Wicket Gate* (1923), and *The Word and the Work* (1925). He worked for the Industrial Christian Fellowship and embarked on speaking tours around Britain. He gave away his possessions and supplemented his modest salary with large royalties from his books – all of which he donated to charities. Kennedy died leaving very little money. As an outspoken ambassador for the working classes, one of his most resonant and, for the established Church, disturbing quotations was:

> If finding God in our churches leads to us losing Him in our factories, then better we tear down those churches, for God must hate the sight of them.
>
> [Bob Holman, *Woodbine Willie: An Unsung Hero of World War One*, 2013, p. 110]

When he died (in Liverpool on a speaking tour) in 1929 at the age of forty-five, 2,000 people flocked to his funeral in Worcester lining the roads from Worcester Cathedral to his old parish church of St Paul's. In a marvellous and apt gesture they tossed packets of Woodbines onto the passing cortege. The plaque inside the cathedral proclaims him as 'A Poet: A Prophet: A Passionate seeker after Truth'. Back in London the Dean of Westminster, remembering what Studdert Kennedy had said about factories and the Church, refused him burial at Westminster Abbey. In 2013, John Packer, Bishop of Ripon and Leeds redeemed the Anglican church when he unveiled a commemorative plaque in Ripon to honour the Ripon Clergy College and Studdert Kennedy.

David Gooderson's *War! Lies! And a Packet of Fags!* tells the story of 'Woodbine Willie'. He gets a mention in Joyce's *Finnegans Wake*: 'tsingirillies' zyngarettes, while Woodbine Willie, so popular with the poppyrossies' (l. 351), and in the Divine Comedy song 'Absent Friends': 'Woodbine Willie couldn't rest until he'd/given every bloke a final smoke/before the killing'. The irony of Woodbine Willie's dichotomy is not lost on Gooderson: espousing war made a hero out of him, but eschewing war and preaching peace attracted all-round vilification. This excerpt from the play is particularly poignant, and one hopes, not too prescient:

> STUDDERT KENNEDY: If we can gather our dead – Germans, Austrians, Russians alike – into one noble brotherhood and make them cry to us a personal cry that nothing can be gained by victory in war by anybody, anytime, anywhere – then there is hope. If not, I fear that, as we grow cleverer, we shall produce more and more monstrous things to maim and kill, until at last in some awful final struggle we shall wreck the world we ought to rule, and die amidst its ruins.

Philip Larkin (1922–1985)

To follow in Larkin's tracks is to take not only a literary journey, but also journeys through diverse landscapes and rich architecture and, seeing the city through a poet's eyes, to gain a philosophical view of the place where Larkin lived and worked for three decades.

The Larkin Trail: Discover a Poet's Landscape,
© Larkin25 2017

When some people think of Philip Larkin, they then think of Hull, the city in which Larkin was librarian at the university. When some people think first of Hull, they then think of Philip Larkin, and then of fish – or perhaps the other way round. Larkin is virtually synonymous with the city; he is literally part of the landscape, or the riverscape, he describes in some of his poetry.

Larkin is not from Hull. He was born and spent his early childhood in Coventry where his father, a Nazi sympathiser and Nuremburg rally veteran, dominated his mother, a chronic sufferer of social anxiety. The good news is that Larkin senior introduced his son to Ezra Pound (well, maybe not in this case – Pound was another Hitler, and Mussolini, sympathiser), T. S. Eliot, James Joyce and D. H. Lawrence and that Larkin junior delighted in his discovery of the Coventry public library. Despite it all, Larkin's parents were supportive of their son and fostered his early love of jazz. While at King Henry VIII Senior School he passed the entrance exams for St John's College, Oxford, to read English and gained a First. 1943 saw Larkin appointed librarian of the public library in Wellington, Shropshire; in 1946, he took the post of librarian at University College, Leicester. In 1950–1955 Larkin was sub-librarian at The Queen's University of Belfast.

Larkin felt at home with the liminal in life. Speaking of Hull, one of England's most liminal of places, he says 'Having got here, it suits me in many ways. It is a little on the edge of things, I think even its natives would say that. I rather like being on the edge of things' [Quoted in 'Aubade' by Philip Larkin by Mark Aldrich, https://thegadabouttown.

com/2016/12/02/aubade-by-philip-larkin/]. This edginess comes over in his poetry, at once reassuring us then, simultaneously almost, biting us when we are off guard. But it is his very own social liminality that helps make him the revered poet that he is: his 'This Be the Verse' famously tell us of parents fucking us all up; he is 'wanking at ten past three', in 'Love Again'; we know from his correspondence of his penchant for pornography; 'Aubade' begins 'I work all day, and get half-drunk at night'.

Arriving in Hull in 1955, Larkin bedsat around before renting a self-contained flat on the top-floor of 32 Pearson Park, 'Carisbrooke', a three-storey house overlooking the park, then owned by the university but previously the home of the American Consulate. This was one of Larkin's high windows, a room with a view of Hull's delightfully Victorian twenty-seven-acre Pearson Park. The view of the park inspired 'Toads Revisited' with its lake, sunshine and grass; and the trees coming into leaf in 'The Trees'.

A low window view of the park from Larkin's house.

Larkin, a conscientious, highly professional and industrious librarian, was personally involved in the design and furnishing of the striking new Brynmor Jones Library around 1967, a building he called the 'lifted study-storehouse'. If in the 1970s he cared to look out of the seventh-floor windows – more high windows – he would see below him a 360° panorama of the campus, Hull's urban landscape and its Humber hinterland, taking in the seemingly endlessly unfinished Humber Bridge as it inched its way to completion. The viewing point in Hessle which he visited when going to the Marvell Press, his early publishers, would have suggested that place where sky, Lincolnshire and water coalesce. Of the bridge itself, he says in Anthony Hedges' cantata 'Bridge for the Living' (1981): 'A giant step for ever to include All our dear landscape in a new design.'

The Brynmor Jones library in 2017.

In his foreword to 'A Rumoured City' (1982) Larkin denies that environment or landscape inspires his poetry: 'A place cannot produce good poems; it can only not prevent them and Hull is good at that. It neither impresses nor insists.' To Larkin, Hull was 'a city that is in the world yet sufficiently on the edge of it to have a different resonance'.

But the intrinsic solitude involved in being on the edge and at the end of the line – these factors that characterise Hull, Holderness, 'lonelier and lonelier', and the Humber – complemented the man – he was independent, private and sometimes, by choice, lonely just like his adopted city. His work was, at least at times, informed by all these qualities, his personal social landscape and the topographical sea, land and urban landscapes all merged to emerge in his poetry. At the same time there was a positive, elevating side to it all: he himself says that alighting from the train at Paragon gave the poet that 'end-of-the-line sense of freedom'.

Life above the park in the 'green-fringed eyrie' came to an end when in 1974 Hull University made plans to sell his building. So, he bought a detached four-bedroomed 1950s house in leafy Newland Park (number 105) opposite the campus on Cottingham Road – a house later described by John Kenyon, warden of Nicholson Hall and friend, as 'an entirely middle-class backwater'[Quoted in R. Hibbett, *Philip Larkin, British Culture, and Four-letter Words*].. More liminality, in Newland Park. Larkin seemed to concur with Kenyon when he said he thought the property 'utterly undistinguished...the ugliest one-roomed house in Hull' and mused on how it might account for the flight of his muse: 'I can't say it's the kind of dwelling that is eloquent of the nobility of the human spirit' [*The Larkin Trail*, http://www.thelarkintrail.co.uk/beyond-the-city-centre.php?item=trialItem_name_17].

Even settings as mundane as library lifts can form part of an exciting literary landscape: Larkin, it must be said, never went out of his way to ingratiate himself with the students of Hull University; like the writer of the graffito below, he was often to be seen in the library lift (his 'lifted study-storehouse') ascending to or descending from his office. Never once did I personally see him smile, although he was not infrequently to be heard chastising his fellow travellers for some inconsiderable trifle. The following insult is extreme and puerile, but many a former student will understand how and why it came to be written:

> PHILIP LARKIN, LIBRARIAN, WAS GREETED at work one morning by a message on the lift wall: 'FUCK OFF LARKIN YOU CUNT'. 'By evening', Larkin grumbled [in a letter]

to his good friend Kingsley Amis, *'the last two words had been erased by some reader of more delicate mind who still agreed with the main thesis. Felt like writing underneath YOU FUCK OFF TOO – LARKIN'*.

[Quoted in R. Hibbett, *Philip Larkin, British Culture, and Four-letter Words*]

I doubt very much that the motive of the graffito chimed much with Hibbett's analysis:

The crassly informal attack, and the mock exchange Larkin makes of it in his letter to Amis, make explicit a conflict already present in Larkin's poetry, where swear words are exclusively linked to generational discord. As in the anecdote above, the profane utterance occurs where social difference is keenly felt, and sharpens the lines between age (Larkin was 58 at the time) and youth, authority and deviance, celebrity and anonymity, and private and public discourse.

[R. Hibbett, *Philip Larkin, British Culture, and Four-letter Words*]

He or she presumably just thought he was lugubrious and saturnine.

In 'The Whitsun Weddings' (1964) Larkin, running late, takes us out of Hull's Paragon Station on a slow train to London running behind the 'backs of houses…smelt the fish dock'; the steamy hot journey punctuated by a series of halts at which various wedding parties throng the platforms. Close by the platform is the mahogany-panelled bar of the Station Hotel. Anyone who has been there knows that you can almost touch the smothering atmosphere of the place, immortalised in Larkin's 'Friday Night at the Royal Station Hotel' (1966) where 'silence laid like carpet'. We've all been there, even if not actually in Hull. The urban landscape recurs in 'Dockery and Son' (1963) when 'A known bell chimes. I catch my train, ignored. Canal and clouds and colleges subside Slowly from view'. He dozes but, when industrial landscape intrudes, is 'waking at the fumes And furnace-glares of Sheffield'. The bustling Newland Avenue streetscape near his house is remembered in *MCMXIV* for 'the shut shops, the bleached Established names on the sunblinds'. Further afield, beautifully remote, wild and desolate Spurn Point was for Larkin where 'ends the land suddenly beyond a beach Of shapes and shingle'.

'Friday Night at the Royal Station Hotel' (1966) where 'silence laid like carpet'.

Marks & Spencer in Whitefriargate, that very ordinary mainstay of many an urban streetscape, gets the Larkin treatment in 'The Large Cool Store' (1961). Impelled by its popularity amongst his staff and their branded carrier bags, Larkin visited, had a good look round and wrote of 'cheap clothes set out in simple sizes plainly...Browns and greys, maroon and navy'. This is Larkin sampling the M&S retail experience, verbalising the retail landscape in all its mundanity.

The poem 'Here' (1961) depicts the Hull that Larkin saw and experienced as he cycled and walked about noting and then versifying his observations with 'Workmen at dawn'; the landscape of 'the widening river's slow presence', and the 'shining gull-marked mud'; the cityscape where 'domes and statues, spires and cranes cluster Beside grain-scattered streets, barge-crowded water, And residents from raw estates' with their

Cheap suits, red kitchen-ware, sharp shoes, iced lollies, Electric mixers, toasters, washers, driers— A cut-price crowd, urban yet simple, dwelling Where only salesmen and relations come Within a terminate and fishy-smelling Pastoral of ships up streets, the slave museum, Tattoo-shops, consulates, grim head-scarfed wives.

All of Hull is here. *Here* is all of Hull.

'The widening river's slow presence'

Larkin sometimes attended trad jazz concerts at the City Hall in Hull; 'Broadcast' finds him in his Pearson Park flat listening to a City Hall symphony broadcast. Trips on the Humber ferry afforded Larkin the chance to experience the riverscape: the 'isolate city spread alongside water' while the city's 'working skyline wanders to the sea'; Hull Royal Infirmary is the building in 'The Building' (1971). Spring Bank Cemetery was for Larkin 'the most beautiful spot in Hull…a natural cathedral' – indeed, an uplifting rural–urban landscape which must have informed the more lugubrious elements of his poetry. The falling leaves and the 'estateful of washing' in 'Afternoons' were inspired by the King George V playing fields in Northgate, Cottingham.

Hull Royal Infirmary is the building in *The Building*.

Inside Ye Olde Black Boy – a Larkin haunt

Mary Linskill (1840–1891)

and while they were sitting there talking quietly together and looking out over the sea, a sharp splinter of rock fell from the top of the cliff, spinning round and round as it fell, and it struck one of the sisters on the back of the neck, so that it took her head quite off.

The Haven under the Hill, 1886

Novelist, short-story writer and poet Mary Linskill was born in Blackburn's Yard, off Church Street in Whitby where her father was a jet-worker and town constable. The landscape, the North seascape and the scenery of Yorkshire runs through much of her work. When her father died the family were left impoverished. Linskill, therefore, left school at the age of twelve and found work as an apprentice milliner in Charles Wilson's shop. She relocated to nearby Newholm-cum-Dunsley and later moved away from Whitby to Manchester and then Newcastle-under-Lyme, became a teacher in Nottingham and a governess in Derby. Writing was her aim and ambition, and eventually one of her serials was published in *Good Words*, a popular magazine of the day for which she became a regular contributor.

In 1871 she published *Tales of the North Riding* (under the pseudonym 'Stephen York'), which, as the title suggests, is redolent of things Yorkshire; this assured her reputation as a writer. *The Haven under the Hill* (1886) gives more of Whitby as well as a perceptive description of the Leeds Music Festival of 1883 which Dorigen, her hero, attends. It also gives a graphic picture of the jet-working industry – a major part of the local economy – and shines a light onto the lives of the jet-workers.

Rock slips were another feature of Whitby life and Linskill has no qualms about describing this macabre and disturbing incident.

During Dorigen's childhood Salvain cautions Dorigen about the safety of the cliffs in the surrounding area:

> The cliff looks frightfully dangerous when you look up from below; indeed it is dangerous. You must never sit down under

it, my dear. Once – it was in the year 1808 – two young Staithes girls, sisters they were, sat down on the scaur – I'll show you the exact spot when we go down – and while they were sitting there talking quietly together and looking out over the sea, a sharp splinter of rock fell from the top of the cliff, spinning round and round as it fell, and it struck one of the sisters on the back of the neck, so that it took her head quite off. The other sister saw it rolling away over the scaur to a great distance before it stopped. Think of that, my dear, whenever you are tempted to sit down under the cliffs. It is quite true, and what has happened once may always happen again.

[*The Haven Under the Hill*, 1928, p. 28]

The story is corroborated in the *Saturday Magazine* for 27 July 1833.

In 1887, *Between the Heather and the Northern Sea* was published and illuminated yet more of nineteenth-century Whitby life. The book includes a story based on one of the most unusual sea rescues ever. In January 1881 the brig *Visitor* foundered off the Bay during a blizzard; the lifeboat crew took to their boat, but were forced to remain outside the harbour. It was impossible to launch the Whitby lifeboat at Whitby and so eighteen horses and 200 or so men from Whitby and Robin Hood's Bay hauled the Whitby boat, *The Robert Whitworth*, the six miles from Whitby to the bay, in snow drifts seven feet deep in places. At the end of the two-hour trek the men lowered the lifeboat down the famously steep street towards the seas with ropes. The first launch had to be aborted – the oars were smashed by a wave. At this point John Skelton, a local man with local knowledge of the Bay, waded in and swam towards the *Visitor*'s crew, plotting a safe route for the lifeboat.

Other works include the 1886 *Hagar: a North Yorkshire Pastoral*, all about Yorkshire coast and country folk; *In Exchange for a Soul: A Novel* (1887) tells how a Yorkshire fisher-girl rises to be the wife of the Squire. Linskill died at Stakesby Vale, Whitby and was initially buried in an unmarked grave. She was known as the 'The Whitby Novelist' or as the 'novelist of the North' whose characters were 'portraits of Northern folk, as they who have lived among them will recognise, and her scenery is precisely what one recalls' [Jan Hewitt, 'The "Haven" and the "Grisly Rokkes": Mary Linskill's Dangerous Landscapes and the Making of Whitby', p. 280].

Andrew Marvell (1621–1678)

But at my back I always hear Time's wingèd chariot hurrying near

Andrew Marvell, 'To His Coy Mistress'

Philip Larkin, Sean O'Brien and Douglas Dunn, of course, are not Hull's only celebrated poets; the metaphysical poet Andrew Marvell was penning poetry in and around the city some 300 years before. Marvell was born in Winestead-in-Holderness, near Hull, the son of a Church of England clergyman. The Marvells moved to Hull when Andrew Marvell Snr was appointed lecturer at Holy Trinity Church there; the younger Marvell went to Hull Grammar School.

Marvell went on to be politician, poet, wit, spy and satirist; with Milton he was Latin Secretary during the Commonwealth, and for about twenty years MP for Hull. Between 1650 and 1652, Marvell was tutor to Mary Fairfax, the daughter of the Lord General Thomas Fairfax, and lived during that time at Nun Appleton Hall, near York, where he got on with writing his poetry, including 'To His Coy Mistress' and 'The Garden'. From 1659 until his death, Marvell was London agent for the Hull Trinity House.

The Bridge Inn, Darfield, August 1964.

Ian McMillan (b. 1956)

Darfield's my tuning fork.

Ian McMillan

To say that Ian McMillan is *the* voice of Yorkshire, with his signature Barnsleyesque accent, would be an understatement. The man is drenched in Yorkshire, a living epitome of the three counties and an ambassador beyond peer for Yorkshireness. McMillan was born in Darfield – four miles from Barnsley – and still lives there. He played drums for 'Oscar the Frog', Barnsley's first folk-rock band. The local pit closed in 1989.

McMillan's prolific work on radio, television, on the stage and in print speaks eloquently for itself and consistently reveals an unmistakeable literary landscape forged by his upbringing and grown-up life in Darfield – a landscape that is all, and always says, Yorkshire. He was educated locally, went to Wath Grammar School and got a degree in Modern Studies from what was then North Staffordshire Polytechnic in 1978. That same decade saw him on the stage performing live poetry. If we need further Yorkshire credentials, he posts a weekly column in *The Barnsley Chronicle*; is 'poet in residence' to Barnsley FC; his play *Sister Josephine Kicks the Habit* (2005) is based on the work of fellow Yorkshireman Jake Thackray; he is Yorkshire Planetarium's Poet in Space and Humberside Police's Beat Poet.

Indeed, to underline his devotion to things South Yorkshire he cites a 'great line of Ted Hughes's where he says "Calderdale's my tuning fork"; well, Darfield's my tuning fork' [www.poetryarchive.org/poet/ian-mcmillan].

SNAPE HILL, DARFIELD.

Snape Hill, Darfield about 1910.

Wit, parody and humour pervade his work but McMillan is no sentimentalist over Yorkshire, nor a Yorkshire nationalist; take these passages from his poetry which show a sometimes harsh realism about Barnsley's place in the world: in 'Visit', set in a hospital room, Barnsley is 'laid out like a stroke victim'; and from 'The Er Barnsley Seascapes': 'Put it this way; / Darfield was mentioned in the Domesday Book. / put it like this: a passing mention, / more of a mutter.' 'The Grimness' satirizes lazy media clichés about life up north and acidly concludes with:

> Do you think I should do that bit at the end again? Let's listen back. A man was trying to breathe in a house two miles away. Bloody deafened me, pal.

> [© Ian McMillan]

In McMillan's work we can see a kaleidoscope of northern, Yorkshire images.

Yorkshire dialect is another enduring love. His 2007 *Chelp and Chunter: a Guide to the Tyke Tongue* is a compendium of Yorkshire dialect words, many of the words in which are native to specific areas of Yorkshire or specific towns or villages. 'The Meaning of Life: A Yorkshire Dialect Rhapsody' demonstrates his ear for the natural cadences of Yorkshire speech patterns.

Barry Hines' *A Kestral for a Nave* was a major influence; McMillan explains why:

> When I was growing up in Darfield near Barnsley in the early 1960s, there weren't many writers who wrote about people who talked like me and lived in the kinds of places I lived in… Then, in my second year at Wath grammar school, Mrs Dove passed me a brand new hardback called A Kestrel for a Knave; 'I think you'll like this,' she said. 'The writer's called Barry Hines and he's from round here. He knows our Keith.'… Hines gave me the confidence to attempt to capture the authentic Yorkshire language on the page. In his books my dour Barnsley minimalism was presented in a celebratory way, in a way that could, if you looked closely, be as nuanced and subtle as what my Auntie Mabel still called The King's English. As I have said before many times in the Yorkshire voice that Hines allowed me to write in, here in the former South Yorkshire coalfield A Kestrel for a Knave is our Moby-Dick, our Things Fall Apart, our Great Gatsby, our Grapes of Wrath.

> **[Ian McMillan, *The Guardian*, 21 March 2016]**

In 2012, to celebrate the UK's National Pie Week, he composed a 'piem' devoted to the 'pie village' of Denby Dale.

The Arsonists is an opera composed by Alan Edward Williams, but it is an opera with a difference: *The Arsonists* is a tale of Yorkshire folk and features South Yorkshire dialect: rehearsals in the summer of 2017 have revealed some problems accommodating the traditional vowel sounds native to the region. Ian McMillan wrote the libretto and describes the work as a 'very exciting experiment' with plenty of 'owts' and 'nowts'.

Fiona Mozley (b. 1988)

I missed the landscape so moved back home to York.

Fiona Mozley

Fiona Mozley is studying for a PhD in medieval studies (specifically, the concept of decay in late-medieval towns and eco-politics) at York University and works in The Little Apple Bookshop in High Petergate at weekends; she was educated at Fulford School in York and at King's College, Cambridge.

The East Coast line from York to London has played a big part in her literary career so far: it was while watching the Yorkshire landscape hurtle by through the train window that she found the inspiration for her debut 2017 novel, *Elmet*, nominated for the Man Booker Prize in the same year.

> 'I wrote the first chapter on the train when my native North Yorkshire whizzed by the window,' she said. 'I missed the landscape so moved back home to York. It took me three years to finish it, writing intermittently.'

> [*York Press*, 28 July 2017]

Daniel, the narrator, describes the elemental nature of Yorkshire and its essence: 'The soil was alive with ruptured stories that cascaded and rotted then found form once more and pushed up through the undergrowth and back into our lives' [*Elmet*].

> Elmet is deeply rooted in the landscape of Mozley's childhood, from the hare standing so still in a field it seems she has 'grabbed hold of the earth and pinned it down with her at its centre', to a winter morning with 'summer scents … bottled by the cold'.

Two of the landscapes Fiona Mozley may have missed

But the novel also bears the marks of the PhD in medieval history she is currently pursuing at York University, with a plot forged by changes in society that have played out in the north of England over hundreds of years. 'There's this community that, at one point, all lived on the land and worked the land, and then were dragged from the land and into the mines or the mills because of the Industrial Revolution,' Mozley says. 'Then the mines and the mills were no longer profitable, so we spat all these people out. But we don't give them back the land, so what do they do?'

[Richard Lea, *Guardian*, 17 August 2017]

The plot revolves around how the borderline-feral Daniel and his sister Cathy live in a house they and their 'Daddy' (something of a cross between a Yorkshire Goliath and Robin Hood) have built – illegally – near the main East Coast rail line in south Yorkshire; inevitably, all sorts of trouble follows. The book is peppered with local dialogue and dialect; its characters are the socially marginalised, repressed and suppressed northerners of the 1980s.

Elmet the place, as in modern Barwick-in-Elmet, Scholes-in-Elmet and Sherburn-in-Elmet, is significant too and is redolent of Yorkshire history; it was an independent Celtic or Brittonic kingdom covering what became roughly the West Riding of Yorkshire in the Early Middle Ages, between the fifth and seventh centuries. Ancient Elmet symbolises Mozley's landscape and terrain.

Landscape for Mozley is inspirational and vital, as these reviews indicate:

Those who have been socio-economically repressed... resurge in this rich, fabular novel, as does something more radical and doomed: a pre-capitalist morality. The embedding of such myths in the language and landscape of [Ted] Hughes, dragged down from the moorland and into the woods, makes for a scarred, black gem.

[Mark Blacklock in *The Guardian*, 9 August 2017]

Canonical influences peep out from behind the book's themes: Thomas Hardy's sense of fateful disaster; D H Lawrence's preoccupation with class and land, and Wuthering Heights, in its outsider spirit and wild Yorkshire landscape — yet none of it is derivative.

[Arifa Akbar in *The Evening Standard*, 3 August 2017]

John Nicholson (1790–1843)

Nicholson also goes by the name of the 'Airedale Poet' or the 'Bingley Byron'. His most enduring work is *Airedale in Ancient Times*. Industrial and rural landscapes around Airedale figure prominently in his writings. He was born in Harewood and moved as a child with the family to Eldwick, near Bingley. His education was unconventional to say the least and made a lasting impression on his work. Nicholson was educated on the moors above Baildon while employed to gather heather and repeating the lessons given to him by the schoolmaster, Mr Briggs. The heather was used to make besoms, as Mr Briggs could not earn enough from teaching to make ends meet.

Aged twelve, he did a year at Bingley Grammar School tutored by Dr Hartley who later edited his *Airedale in Ancient Times*. At thirteen, he was working in his father's mill as a woolcomber. By night he read avidly: Milton, Shakespeare and Pope were all illuminated by candlelight and when his mother confiscated his candles, he made his own from a mustard pot, a cotton cord for a wick and olive oil to burn. His father would read the classic works to the family around the fireplace. As an adolescent he trekked the moors around Eldwick, reading or playing his hautboy. In 1818, he moved his second wife and their children to Red Beck where he took work in Shipley Fields Mill; during his time here he was commissioned to write two plays, *The Robber of the Alps* and *The Siege of Bradford*, based on the civil war.

A tireless Nicholson travelled the north-east and journeyed to London to sell these books. The family eventually moved to Saltaire and Nicholson began working for Sir Titus Salt. Other published poems include: 'The Lyre of Ebor'; 'Airedale's Beauties'; 'Bingley's Beauties'; 'Mary of Marley'; 'An Old Oak Tree in Bradford'; 'On Visiting a Workhouse'; 'The Vale of Ilkley'; 'The Malt Inn Fire'; 'A Place of Rural Retirement'; 'The Vale of Ilkley'; 'The New Church at Wilsden'; 'Appeal of the Spanish Refugees'; 'Elegy on the Death of Lord Byron'; and 'On a Young Lady Drowned in the Strid'. All drew on the experiences and reflections of the young Nicholson on the moors above Baildon and the surrounding region. An example of his vivid industrial landscape poetry comes in

> When first the shapeless sable ore Is laid in heaps around Low Moor, The roaring blast, the quiv'ring flame, Give to the mass another name: White as the sun the metal runs, For horse-shoe nails, or thund'ring guns...No pen can write, no mind can soar To tell the wonders of Low Moor.
>
> [John Nicholson , 'Low Moor Iron Works', *The Poetical Works of John Nicholson ... (the Airedale Poet)* 1876]

A play, *Poetry or Bust*, was written about Nicholson by Tony Harrison and premiered in 1993 in Salts Mill. It is a tragi-comedy that tells the life and death of Nicholson. Tony Harrison has a bust of John Nicholson in his house.

Sean O'Brien (b. 1952)

Let North, from Humber's shore to Tweed / Exist in verse, if not yet deed.

'A Northern Assembly', 2001

Sean O'Brien grew up in Hull, was educated at Selwyn College, Cambridge, and currently teaches at the University of Newcastle-upon-Tyne. He was born in decidedly un-North Holland Park but the family moved within the year to Hull, a place he remembers as being wet:

> Since childhood, water has been an excitement. The city was built on a swamp: if you dug a hole in your back yard, the water would rise up to look back at you. We fished for sinister-looking minnows in the old storm drains, which grew great mats of algae, thick as hearth rugs, on top of black, jelly-like water. The cellars of the pubs down by the river were said to flood, which presumably had some sort of effect on the beer. And everybody smoked, so everybody had bronchitis, so people were sitting barking in damp doctors' surgeries ... There was a half-amphibian feel to the place. Water was inescapable.

> [*The Guardian*, 14 August 2009]

A very wet, but fun, Hull

As far as the influence of Hull is concerned, he himself is eloquent on how his upbringing forged indelible and elemental urban landscapes and riverscapes in his poetry:

> I grew up in a northern city, and the landscape fascinates me: the flat, Saxon plains of east Yorkshire, the spectacular hills of the north and west, the uncompromising industrial cities – they form a complex identity. And they all touch on the Humber – the great, epic, Mississippianly wide river Humber – which runs past the doorstep like a continental division and moves out vastly into the sea. When we were kids, we used to think we could see palm trees on the other side. [The north is] where my loyalty lies: friends, family, politics.

> [*The Guardian*, 14 August 2009]

'From Cockermouth to Withernsea', he says in 'A Northern Assembly' from *Downriver* and in *Downriver* he says, 'The North – the North is poetry'. Fiona Sampson, editor of *Poetry Review*, calls this working of place and verse with its brown river, railway lines, trade unions and big skies 'a psychic landscape'. Hull and the north, then, pervades his poetry, it is an essential component of his work, it is a ubiquitous O'Brien place.

Hymer's College.

O'Brien passed the entrance exam to Hull's Hymer's College in (then) leafy Sunny Bank, a school that had a profound influence on him and his poetry: it was 'an extremely good education, very old-fashioned – grammar, maths, Latin. I've always felt the benefit of it' [Sarah Crown, *Guardian*, 14 August 2009]. An 'electric light moment' came in 1967 when O'Brien's English teacher handed out copies of poetry books by Ted Hughes and T. S. Eliot:

> A light went on. This was the most interesting thing I'd ever encountered. Eliot was so powerfully grim, atmospheric, authoritative; Hughes's early poems made the physical world look more substantial. And that was it, really: I decided that was how I was going to occupy my time. It's from then that I date my serious, conscious involvement in trying to write poems.
>
> [Ibid.]

As the couplet at the head of this chapter reveals in a kind of prologue to *Downriver*, O'Brien's goal is to versify his personal version of the North. His experiences of Hull (and Newcastle) inform the poems in the collection: the landscapes he creates are shaped by a childhood in Hull.

When writing about *Cousin Coat: Selected Poems 1976–2001* (2002), in the *PBS Bulletin*, O'Brien outlines the sense of place that inspired many of the poems: 'beginning in the half-bombed Victorian streets of Hull in the 1950s, taking in its hidden gardens, parks, railways and the vast presence of the Humber estuary'. These (and other northern places) have been elevated and include rich maritime imagery, 'tides in the paper', 'dry sailors', and characters 'heading out on a snow boat / To sail off the compass for home' ('Terra Nova'). Hull, as we have seen, is a place with a 'closeness to water / That water is bearing away' ('From the Whalebone'), reaching a climax in *The Drowned Book* (2007).

As with Larkin, the parkscape furnished by Hull's Pearson Park is evident in the poetry. As Jules Smith says in a British Council essay that underscores the importance of landscape and dreamscape in O'Brien's work:

O'Brien's first poetic territory was 'urban pastoral', exemplified by the front cover photograph of his first collection, The Indoor Park (1983), showing an opened door in the Victorian Conservatory in Pearson Park, Hull (a leafy space in the inner city, adjacent to his childhood home). This conservatory appears in various guises throughout his poetry, most surreally as a submarine, the 'Unterseebot of the state' in HMS Glasshouse (1991), with 'its vaulted heat, / its bleared below-decks light'. The park itself, significantly for O'Brien a creation of Victorian civic ambition, appears regularly in his dreamscapes, as in Ghost Train (1995), where 'The dead are reassembling, / There beneath the dripping trees / Beside the pond' ('Revenants').

[https://literature.britishcouncil.org/writer/sean-obrien]

Pearson parkscape.

O'Brien explains how The Drowned Book poems 'began with a childhood memory of digging a hole in the back garden [in Hull] and seeing water gradually rising to fill it' [Emma Townshend, Independent on Sunday, 10 February 2008] reminding us of 'Water-

Gardens', whose opening is an image of water looking 'up through the lawn / Like a half-buried mirror', and proceeds to the 'rot-smelling Boulevard mansions' – an allusion to the leafy Hull Avenues opposite Pearson Park. Round the corner at the top of Spring Bank, the Polar Bear pub is the setting for 'Those in Peril'.

The Polar Bear pub.

Hull

Alan Plater (1935–2010)

The north was so damn fashionable. I used to be a cool guy. When I started coming down to London for meetings, I flattened my vowels more and played it up. 'I love the way you talk,' people would say. And I'd say, 'Oh aye?' I wasn't the smooth sophisticate you see before you now.

Alan Plater

Alan Plater, playwright and TV screenwriter, was born in Jarrow; the family moved to Hull in 1938 where he attended Kingston High School; here he met Tom Courtenay who became a lifelong friend. Plater's father worked for the London and North Eastern Railway in charge of a blacksmith's shop off Hessle Road. Later in life, when success had made him comfortable, Alan Plater lived on leafy Westbourne Avenue opposite Pearson Park.

Comfortable Westbourne Avenue.

Joan Littlewood, the theatre director, was a major influence: she told Plater the aspiring playwright, in a reference to the musicality of the local accent, that 'You can walk the streets of Hull and hear the people talking poetry'. He attributes his love of the theatre and a passion for social and cultural landscapes to Hull's 'Tivoli' – a Victorian music hall, long gone, 'in whose wings Old Mother Riley breathed her last – and by the local rep theatre, in which he watched plays about Home Counties families who never went to work and drank gin in the afternoons' [*Independent*, 4 September 2004]. Littlewood and a touring production of *Look Back in Anger* changed all that. His affinity with the urban landscapes of Hull and Newcastle never left him and are evidenced in plays such as *Close the Coalhouse Door* and *Land of Green Ginger*, a street in Hull's Old town (1973).

After dodging National Service, Plater took a job in a Hull architect's office: 'I did all the crappy jobs that nobody wanted to do. I ended up measuring fields in Thorngumbald [eight miles east of Hull], after which they were filled with nasty semi-detached bungalows' [ibid.].

Alan Plater was a fervent supporter of Hull City. His play *Confessions of a City Supporter* charts his lifelong love of the club and was staged as one of the first ever performances at the new home of the Hull Truck Theatre. He had helped establish the Spring Street Theatre, home to John Godber's Hull Truck company. *Confessions* describes the Tigers' centenary with a story of four generations of men born on the days of scoreless draws.

Of the surreal north–south divide play, *The Incident,* he says that

> It was one of my first overtly political dramas...The proposition was that because of the growing unemployment and deprivation in the north of England they'd actually built a kind of wall across the country and this was about people who were trying to infiltrate over the border. It was very strange and weird...

[http://www.screenonline.org.uk/people/id/473028/index.html]

Other northern inflected dramas included *Z Cars* set in Lancashire, *The Villains* set in the North West and *The Nutter* – one of a trilogy of plays called *Portraits From The North*; the six-part *Trinity Tales* (1975), an update of Chaucer's *Canterbury Tales* featuring a group of rugby league supporters travelling to a Wembley cup final and *The Fosdyke Saga* (1977), a northern parody of *The Forsyte Saga* with the cartoonist Bill Tidy.

A scene from the Humber

Sylvia Plath (1932–1963)

I felt my lungs inflate with the onrush of scenery—air, mountains, trees, people. I thought, 'This is what it is to be happy.'

Sylvia Plath, *The Bell Jar*

Sylvia Plath was an American poet, novelist, and short story writer born in Boston, Massachusetts: she was educated at Smith College in Northampton, Massachusetts, and Newnham College, Cambridge. She was married to Ted Hughes from 1956 until 1962. Sylvia Plath committed suicide in 1963; she is buried in Heptonstall parish churchyard of St Thomas the Apostle.

Landscape poetry is ever-present in Plath's work from all stages of her short and tragic life; nowhere more so than in the poems inspired by her West Yorkshire visits to her in-laws. Landscape poetry has been described as 'a rich and important area of her work that is often overlooked ... some of the best of which was written about the Yorkshire moors' [Owen Sheers, https://subsaga. com/bbc/documentaries/arts/a-poets-guide-to-britain/2-sylvia-plath.html]. For example, her 1961 poem 'Wuthering Heights' obviously owes its title to the Emily Brontë novel, but Plath's own individual and personal vision of the brooding Pennine landscape is clearly evident.

Plath was the subject of an episode of BBC4's *A Poet's Guide to Britain;* presenter Owen Sheers puts the landscape poetry into context:

> [Poet and author Owen Sheers] visits the dramatic country around Heptonstall where the newly married Plath came to meet her in-laws, a world of gothic architecture and fog-soaked landscapes, where the locals have a passion for ghost stories that connect directly with the tales that were told in the kitchen of the Bronte parsonage. His journey eventually leads out onto the high moors and the spectacular ruin known as Top Withens. Here amongst the wind and sheep

'where the grass is beating its head distractedly', Plath found the material for some of her most impressive writing.

[BBC4, *A Poet's Guide to Britain*, episode 4, 28 July 2013]

'November Graveyard' is about the meaning of death:

a poem describing trees, grass, flowers—which 'stubbornly resists mourning over death. But it does not deny death; the visitor notes the 'honest rot' which reveals nature's unsentimental presentation of death and decay. And the poet concludes that this 'essential' landscape may teach us the truth about death... this poem may be seen to exemplify a minor change in her depiction of landscapes; elements of nature are discreetly anthropomorphized: 'skinflint' trees refuse to mourn or 'wear sackcloth,' the 'dour' grass is not willing to put on richer colors to solemnize the place, and the flowers do not pretend to give voice to the dead.*

The old dilapidated church at Heptonstall. Plath is buried nearby.

'The Snowman on the Moor' and 'Two Views of Withens', use moorland as the canvas for 'descriptions of relationships between people and of attitudes to nature'. The latter offers 'two very different attitudes to nature… epitomized in two persons' differing responses to a bare landscape and a dilapidated farmhouse with literary and romantic associations'. To the speaker of the poem, landscape and sky are bleak and 'the House of Eros' is no 'palace'.*

> 'Hardcastle Crags' gives a harsher view of a human being alone and defenseless in an unresponsive, 'absolute' landscape. The poem derives its power from a very detailed, realistic picture of fields and animals, stones and hills. The last Yorkshire poem written in 1957, however, with the title 'The Great Carbuncle,' brings in an element of wonder performed by nature: a certain strange light with magical power—its source remains unknown—creates a moment of transfiguration for the wanderers. The Great Carbuncle may allude to a drop of blood in the Holy Grail. But it is a painfully brief moment: afterwards 'the body weighs like stone.'*

The moors above Haworth.

We return to 'Wuthering Heights', written in 1961, in which Plath revisits 'the ambiguous fascination this moor landscape held for her' but now with a decidedly sinister twist…

> The solitary wanderer bravely 'step[s] forward,' but nature is her enemy: the alluring horizons 'dissolve' at her advance, wind and heather try to undo her. Images of landscape and animals are consistently turned into metaphors for the human intruder's feeling of being insignificant and exposed. A seemingly harmless thing such as the half-closed eyes of the grandmotherly-looking sheep makes the speaker lose her sense of identity and worth… This landscape is indeed 'psychic' … most certainly a result of Plath's greater ability to transform realistic, concrete objects and scenes into consistent sets of metaphors for her thoughts and emotions.*

* For most of these analyses I am indebted to 'Sylvia Plath's Psychic Landscapes' by Brita Lindberg-Seyersted, *English Studies* 71, No. 6, 1990, pp. 509–522 – 'which examines the development of Plath's poetry through analysis of major themes and imagery found in her description of landscapes, seascapes, and the natural world'.

Hubberholme and St Michael & All Angels.

J. B. Priestley (1894–1984)

These Yorkshire Dales are…the most rewarding countryside I have ever known. Is this simply local patriotism or the memory of early enchanted days? It is not…You have come down from Wuthering Heights into Arcadia.

J. B. Priestley, *Life International*, 1966

John Boynton Priestley was born at 5 Mannheim Road, Manningham, which he describes as an 'extremely respectable' suburb of Bradford. His father was a headmaster, the son of an illiterate mill worker; Priestley's mother died when he was two years old. He was educated at Whetley Lane Primary School and, with the help of a scholarship, Belle Vue Grammar School in Manningham Lane. But school bored him and when he left at sixteen he went to work (from 1910 to 1914) as a junior clerk at Helm & Co., a wool firm in Bradford's grand Swan Arcade. So enamoured was he with the arcade that he titled the first part of his literary reminiscences, *Margin Released* (1962), 'The Swan Arcadian'. While at Helm & Co. (1910–1914), he joined the Labour Party and started writing after work; he had articles published in *The Bradford Pioneer* and in London newspapers.

Bradford and its cityscape was to feature prominently in much of his work after he moved south, not least *Bright Day* and *When We Are Married*. In later life he campaigned against the mindless destruction of Bradford's Victorian buildings such as the glorious Swan Arcade demolished in 1962 to be replaced by the usual anonymous brutalist box of glass and concrete.

In the *Heaton Review* (1931) he describes hometown Bradford as

> Not really a town at all; it is a vast series of pictures, in time and space; it is an autobiographical library; it is a hundred thousand succeeding states of mind; it is my childhood and youth; it is a lost world…Bradford itself is ugly and forbidding, and yet within the easiest reach…is some of the loveliest country in England.

Priestley's industrial Bradford.

These sentiments were echoed three years later in his influential and landmark *English Journey* (p. 166). In the same travelogue Beverley is described as 'towering in that pretty rustic flatness'. Hull 'has an air of prosperity…but if atmosphere is more truthful than statistics – then Hull has been fortunate'; 'Leeds is rather more civilised than Bradford…it is a large, dirty town'; 'Sheffield, far below, looked like the interior of an active volcano…the smoke was so thick that it made a foggy twilight in the descending streets, which appeared as if they would end in the steaming bowels of the earth…we were now in true North country'.

After war service Priestley went up to Trinity Hall, Cambridge, reading for a degree in Modern History and Political Science and writing for the *Cambridge Review*. By the time he was thirty he was winning for himself a reputation as an essayist and critic with columns in *the Daily News, The Spectator, The Bookman, The Saturday Review*, and *The Times Literary Supplement*.

The picaresque *The Good Companions* (1929) finds the aging, discontented Jess Oakroyd languishing in the Yorkshire town of Bruddersford (Bradford + Huddersfield). He decides to up and go, to leave his family and seek adventure 'on t'road'. Priestley uses dialect for all non-received pronunciation speakers of English throughout the novel. Jess heads south down the Great North Road.

Nostalgia for pre-World War I north of England is one of the main undercurrents in *Bright Day* (1946), informed by Priestley's Bradford upbringing. It is set in 1946, when an English screenwriter, Gregory Dawson, resides at a seaside hotel, the Royal Ocean, in Tralorna in Cornwall to complete work on a screenplay. A chance meeting with two elderly people from way back when leads him to delve into memories of his youth in Bruddersford between October 1912 and the outbreak of the First World War. We hear about, for example, a day out to the village of Bulsden, on the edge of Broadstone Moor, for a picnic and a game of cricket and another (fateful) picnic at Pikeley Scar.

Priestley's 1937 play, *Time and the Conways,* is notable for being one of his 'Time' plays, deploying J. W. Dunne's Theory of Time as described in his An *Experiment with Time* (1927). The Conways are a moneyed Yorkshire family between 1919 and 1937, wealthy Yorkshire folk who typify the crass complacency and class arrogance he saw pervading Britain between 1919 and 1937: huge creative and humanistic potential was going to waste as the country bumbled towards 'the next war'.

The sitting room of Alderman Helliwell's House in Clecklewyke, a fictional town in the north of England, is the setting for Priestley's 1938 play, *When We are Married: A Yorkshire Farcical Comedy*, in which three couples discover, to their horror, that they are not actually legally married. Press intrusion into subsequent events is provided by the *Yorkshire Argus'* drink-fuelled photographer.

The Yorkshire landscape – rural and industrial – naturally features in Priestley's *English Journey* (1934) – a landmark travelogue that captured the essence of Depression-plagued England. Priestley exposes the country's acute social problems and lobbies for democratic socialist change. *English Journey* was an inspiration for Orwell's *The Road to Wigan Pier*, and 'has even been credited with winning the 1945 election for the Labour Party' [Margaret Drabble, *The Guardian*, 26 January 2008].

Second World War morale-boosting journalism, often in *Picture Post*, included one article, titled 'This Problem of Coal' for which Priestley visited Markham Main colliery at Armthorpe in south Yorkshire on 20 June 1941; the point of the article was to underline the strategic importance of coal and of the people who mined it. Armthorpe village, he found, had almost 1,000 colliery houses creating a community, as with other mining villages, virtually cut off from the rest of the county and country. The following is typical of what he discovered on his visit:

> One miner Priestley met had just finished his shift. He had risen that morning at half past four, had gone down and hewn out 10 to 11 tons of coal. His mid-morning snack, or snap, was a slice or two of bread with a scrape of margarine and a slice of lettuce. After a shower at the colliery baths he had gone home to a dinner of fried potatoes and rice pudding. The miner had not eaten meat since the previous weekend.

> [*Yorkshire Post*, 11 January 2016]

J. B. Priestley painting near Ribblehead [Marie Hartley].
© Dalesman Publishing Company.

Priestley's real love was for the Yorkshire Dales, of which he, a veteran global traveller, writes:

> For variety of landscape these Dales cannot be matched on this island or anywhere else. A day's walk among them will give you almost everything fit to be seen on this earth.

[From his 'Introduction' to *The Beauty of Britain*, 1935]

Two years after his death in 1984, the ashes of J. B. Priestley were scattered in the St Michael & All Angels churchyard in Wensleydale's Hubberholme. He described Hubberholme as 'one of the smallest, pleasantest places in the world' [*The Other Place*, 1953]. The church is next to the wonderful seventeenth-century largely un-modernised George Inn – a favourite Priestley refuge. Elsewhere, he described Hubberholme as 'Hubberholme – just bridge, an inn and a church, all old – is sheer magic, not quite in this world' [*Life International*, 1966].

The Wharfe near Buckden.

Dorothy Una Ratcliffe (1887–1967)

a remarkable woman with a passion for the wild landscapes of the Yorkshire Dales and Westmorland and the birds and wildflowers within them [she]wrote many books, poems, plays and stories about Yorkshire and Westmorland, often in dialect.

The National Trust

In the Leeds City Museum there is a serene but powerful bronze of a woman reading: it is Dorothy Una Ratcliffe, niece of Lord Brotherton and writer of poetry in Yorkshire dialect. She is one of the celebrated (but often overlooked) women poets of the First World War; an example of her work is *Julian Hunter, Soldier Poet – An Idyll in the Dales* [collected in L. London, *Female Poets of the First World War – Volume 2*, 2016]. She helped Lord Brotherton equip the Leeds Old Pals Regiment; a fluent French speaker, she also assisted with settling Leeds' quota of Belgian refugees.

Dorothy Una Ratcliffe (often known simply as DUR) was a flamboyant, colourful and bohemian woman; she published forty-nine books, travelled the world, tended her garden, loved Yorkshire and its traditions, was a prolific collector and inspired a magnificent legacy to the city of Leeds. She was raised in Sussex and Surrey, the eldest of the three daughters of George Benson Clough, a rich barrister from Scarborough: she called him the first Yorkshireman in her life; the author of several books himself, he encouraged her early literary efforts.

In London in 1909, aged twenty-two, she married Charles Frederick Ratcliffe, nephew and heir of the Leeds chemical tycoon Edward Allen Brotherton, later Lord Brotherton of Wakefield, a childless widower. The newly married couple settled in a house near Edward Brotherton's home at Roundhay Hall (later the Spire Hospital), and eventually moved in to the hall themselves. Brotherton and Ratcliffe shared a love for literature and fine books; he underwrote her literary magazine, 'The Microcosm', which featured articles by writers like Tolkien and Chesterton; she helped him build up a magnificent library of rare and precious books and manuscripts, later bequeathed to Leeds University 'in trust for the Nation', and now housed in the Brotherton Library which he had endowed.

Yockenthwaite, upstream from Hubberholme.

Ratcliffe developed a deep love for the Yorkshire Dales, their landscape, dialect and traditions, and in 1918 published her first volume of lyrical, romantic Dales ballads, *The Dales of Arcady* (after Keats's Grecian urn) followed year after year with poems, plays, memoirs, all based on Dales life, some in local dialect and some for children. Poems include 'White Dog of Yockenthwaite'; 'Mad Old Mike'; 'Croodle Beck'; and 'April in Wensleydale'. Her near-obsession with the Romanies and their culture led to works on gypsy life written in what she termed the old ballad tradition. Her gypsy poems, 'Brough Hill Fair' and 'Yorkshire Gypsy' are examples. In the 1920s with her marriage to wayward Charles on the rocks, and determined not to divorce lest the scandal damage Lord Brotherton's political career, Dorothy bought a small country house, Laverton Grange, in Kirby Malzeard, near Ripon, from where she could explore the Dales at will.

Littondale.

Ratcliffe was always an active supporter of the Yorkshire Dialect and Gypsy Lore societies, and remained faithful to the Brotherton Library, to which she donated her collection of Romany material. The Leeds Museum holds her collection of fans and miniatures, and, sadly, baby bonnets – she was unable to bear children thanks to complications from a so-called cure for a sexually transmitted infection caught from her first husband.

Typical of the poverty Seebohm Rowntree would have seen in Walmgate, York

Benjamin Seebohm Rowntree (1871–1954)

I see little glory in an Empire which can rule the waves and is unable to flush its sewers.

Winston Churchill, 1901, alluding to Seebohm Rowntree's *Poverty*

Seebohm Rowntree was born in elegant Bootham in York, the second son of the Quaker Joseph Rowntree; from the age of ten he went to the Quaker Bootham School, then studied chemistry at Owen's

College, Manchester, before joining the family chocolate firm in 1889. Seebohm Rowntree was heavily influenced by his father's substantial, published work in pursuit of social reform to help the poor of York, not least his 1863 statistical study on the links between crime and poverty; *Pauperism in England and Wales* (1865) and *The Temperance Problem and Social Reform* (1900).

Seebohm took up the mantle; his aim was to illuminate York's poverty blighted urban landscape, 'throw some light upon the conditions which govern the life of the wage-earning classes in provincial towns'; to assess 'how much of it [poverty] was due to insufficiency of income, and how much to improvidence'. Indeed, 'the question was not what poverty was, but what were the causes of people living in a state of poverty' [B. S. Rowntree, *Poverty, A Study of Town Life*]. In doing so he would also diligently and meticulously expose the shocking housing and health conditions of the urban poor in York.

Poverty in York

To make the research meaningful and rigorous

> nothing short of a house-to-house inquiry extending to the whole of the working class population of the city would suffice ... to obtain information regarding the housing, occupation and earnings of every wage-earning family in York, together with the number and age of the children in each family.
>
> [ibid.]

In the event, 11,560 families (46,754 individuals) from 388 streets were questioned and provided the seed-corn for Seebohm's landmark *Poverty: A Study of Town Life* (1901). Focussing on the Hungate and Walmgate areas, he describes them as typical of urban slum life: 'reckless expenditure of money as soon as obtained, with the aggravated want at other times; the rowdy Saturday night, the Monday morning pilgrimage to the pawn shop ... the despair of so many social workers' [ibid.]. Establishing a scientifically-based poverty line – 'the income required by families of different sizes to provide the minimum of food, clothing and shelter needful for the maintenance of merely physical health' [ibid.], Rowntree found that 27.84 per cent of the total population of York lived below his poverty line – and 43.4 per cent of the working population (1,465 families). Here is an example of what he and his researchers found:

A married bricklayer's labourer lived in two rooms with wife and three young children:

> the stench here is abominable. The grating of the street drain is 1½ yards from the house door, and is blocked up. There are twenty-three houses in this yard and only one water tap ... four houses join at one closet. There is one ash pit for this yard; it is full to the top, and slime running down the wall. Rent 2s 3d.

Further York poverty studies followed: *Poverty and Progress* (1936) and *Poverty and the Welfare State* (1951). *Unemployment: A Social Study* was published in 1911; *English Life and Leisure: A Social Study* came in 1951.

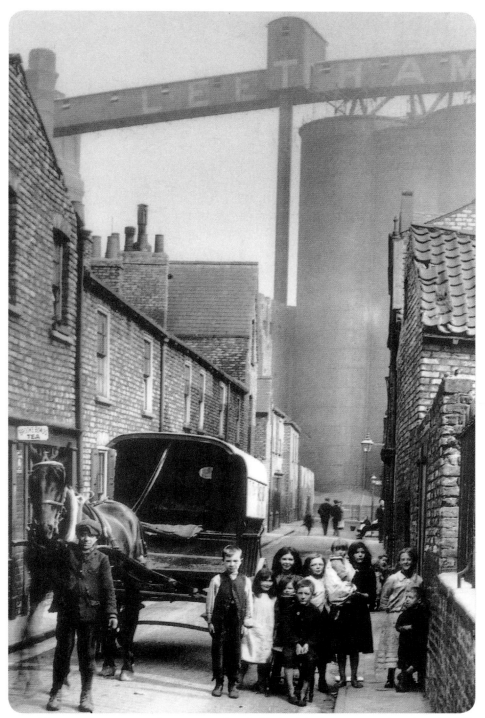

Yet more poverty and overcrowding in York, this time next to Leetham's Mill.

Laurence Sterne (1713–1768)

I take a simple view of life. It is keep your eyes open and get on with it.

Laurence Sterne

Sterne is famous for his *The Life and Opinions of Tristram Shandy, Gentleman*, and the equally witty *A Sentimental Journey Through France and Italy*. Tristram says he is writing a 'civil, nonsensical, good-humoured Shandean book'; 'Shandy' is an obscure word meaning 'crack-brained, half-crazy'. Educated at Hipperholme (now Grammar) School, Halifax, Sterne followed his father and became an Anglican clergyman with a vicarship at Sutton-on-the-Forest, a living at Stillington – both villages are just north of York – and was a prebendary of York Minster, lodging at Hildyard's in Stonegate. Sterne married Elizabeth Lumley who lived in York's College Street close to the Minster. He mines his ecclesiastical landscape and hinterland in his satire, *A Political Romance* (1759), a skit on ecclesiastical disputes at York, where it was suppressed and burnt by outraged churchmen. The infighting exposed by Sterne undoubtedly continues to this day.

Hildyard's in Stonegate – at the sign of the Bible. Just as eccentric today.

The commercial and critical success of the first two volumes of *Tristram Shandy* spawned an equally successful spin-off: two volumes of sermons attributed to Parson Yorick (1760), the village parson introduced in volume one of *Tristram Shandy*, expatiating on his experiences as a priest. As a witty, jocular and misunderstood clergyman, Yorick is said to be a thinly disguised Sterne, who in turn is drawing on twenty years as a Yorkshire country vicar and Minster prebendary. Sterne was reputed to be a gifted giver of sermons in his own parishes and he was frequently engaged to preach from the pulpit of York Minster, even delivering the sermon at the enthronement of Archbishop Herring in 1743. His qualifications to compose the Yorick sermons are, therefore, impeccable. Over time they outsold the bestselling *Tristram Shandy* in terms of lifetime editions, having been marketed to tap into the commercial success of the novel. Two further volumes followed in 1766; three more were posthumously published in 1769.

York Minster.

York's Red House.

Real, actual York people feature in *Tristram Shandy*: Dr John Burton, Catholic and Jacobite sympathiser, was a one-time resident in York's Red House and the model for Sterne's Dr Slop, '... a little squat, uncourtly figure ... about four feet and a half perpendicular height, with a breadth of back, and a sesquipedality of belly, which might have done honour to a serjeant in the horse-guards' [*The Life and Opinions of Tristram Shandy, Gentleman*]. Burton, a gynaecologist educated at Cambridge, Leiden and Rheims, authored the classic *An Essay Towards a Complete System of Midwifery* (1751), illustrated by no less an artist than George Stubbs who had come to York (then, as now, a centre of excellence in medical science) to learn his anatomy. Stubbs found work teaching medical students in the Medical School before taking up comparative anatomy, and painting his famous horses. His most celebrated, *Whistlejacket*, was painted in 1762 and featured the very same horse that won the four-mile chase for 2000 guineas at York's Knavesmire in August 1759. Burton also started the unfinished *Monasticon Eboracense*, an ecclesiastical history of Yorkshire, in 1758. He was incarcerated in York Castle after his involvement in the 1745 Jacobite Rebellion as 'a suspicious person to His Majesty's government' [ibid.]. There is a memorial to him in Holy Trinity Church, Micklegate, York. Burton was also a friend of Jacobite heroine Flora MacDonald – the brave woman who hid Bonnie Prince Charlie on Benbecula after Culloden. She escaped from the Hanoverian militia, which was led by her stepfather, Hugh MacDonald, with a servant, an Irish spinning maid, Betty Burke, and a six-man crew. With all this going on around Sterne in real life it is not surprising to see his hero immersed in so many scrapes and adventures.

Burton's alter ego, Dr Slop, was the local male midwife, who assisted at Tristram's birth with his 'vile instruments' and 'obstetrical engines', a 'scientifick operator' [ibid.]. Dr Slop was the author of a book delineating his scorn for the modern practice of midwifery. Slop's interests lay in surgical instrumentation and medical advances; he prided himself as inventor of a new type of delivery forceps.

Library records show that Sterne was one of 200 or so borrowers at the celebrated Minster Library who made 1,242 loans from 1716 to 1820. Francis Hildyard's shop was established 'at the sign of The Bible' in 1682 and was York's oldest bookseller. Working from home, as it were, Sterne had the first two volumes of *Life and Times of Tristram Shandy, Gentleman* published at 'the Sign of the Bible'. 'The Sign of the Bible' is above 35 Stonegate.

Sterne died of pleurisy in London in 1768; he was buried in the churchyard in Coxwold, but only after a decidedly eventful circuitous journey... having been originally interred in St George's churchyard, Hanover Square, London. His body was snatched from there by 'resurrection men' and sent for use in medical dissection at Cambridge University. The celebrated cadaver was recognised by the Professor of Anatomy who apparently fainted when he saw it on the table and had it hastily reburied. In 1969 the Lawrence Sterne Society obtained permission to remove Sterne's remains to Coxwold for re-burial where they now rest in peace.

Even on a sunny, blue-sky day the consecrated space
around St Mary's looks, and feels, foggy.

Bram Stoker (1847–1912)

*the master of a particularly lurid and creepy kind of fiction, represented by Dracula and other novels.**

'Death of Mr Bram Stoker', *The Times*, 22 April 1912

Abraham 'Bram Stoker' has provided us with one of the England's famous and haunting Yorkshire literary landscapes by making Whitby the setting for his famous Gothic novel, *Dracula,* published in 1897. The associations live on to this day with the terrifying 'Dracula Experience', spooky Dracula walks with commentary, a Bram Stoker Film Festival, productions of *Dracula* in the Abbey ruins, and an annual Goth weekend that fills the town with wonderful Goth costumes, Goth makeup, Goth music and, of course, unfettered Gothic fear. All of this is comparatively easy to achieve due to the unique ambience and aura of Whitby – an atmosphere that would have shrouded Stoker on his morning walks and that remains to this day.

The chapters set in Whitby (six to eight) are the product of Stoker's impressive knowledge and affection for the charming seaport, which he first visited in 1885, followed by other visits until 1890. Staying at Mrs Veazey's guesthouse at 6 Royal Crescent, he also took in the delightful harbours of Ravenscar and Robin Hood's Bay, fourteen miles and five miles south of Whitby respectively.

By 1885 Whitby had a reputation as a very pleasant seaside town and as something of a writers' colony, playing host to the likes of Charles Dickens, Wilkie Collins and Henry James – all looking for land- and seascape inspiration. Whitby has both in spades – whichever way you look and wherever you are. For the name of his creation, Count Dracula, Stoker had to look no further than in a book he was browsing in Whitby library, then at the Coffee House End of the Quay. The book was William Wilkinson's *An Account of the Principalities of Wallachia and Moldavia* published in 1820; Wilkinson had been British consul in Bucharest. Significantly, Wilkinson referred to a fifteenth-century prince called Vlad Tepes who was in the habit of impaling his enemies on wooden stakes. He was called Dracula – the 'son of the dragon'. A footnote further informed Stoker that:

> Dracula in the Wallachian language means Devil. The Wallachians at that time … used to give this as a surname to any person who rendered himself conspicuous either by courage, cruel actions, or cunning.

Stoker would have heard of the shipwreck five years earlier of a Russian vessel called the *Dmitry*, from Narva. The ship ran aground on Tate Hill Sands below East Cliff, carrying a cargo of silver sand. These names fall easily into the *Demeter* from Varna – the Russian schooner *en route* to London that carried Dracula to Whitby laden with a cargo of silver sand and boxes of Transylvanian earth. She ran aground on Tate Hill Sands, crew missing, its dead skipper lashed to the wheel. This is how Stoker describes the *Demeter* making landfall at Whitby with Dracula, in the guise of a huge hound, bounding ashore:

> But, strangest of all, the very instant the shore was touched, an immense dog sprang up on deck from below … and running forward, jumped from the bow on to the sand. Making straight for the steep cliff, where the churchyard hangs over the laneway to the East Pier … it disappeared in the darkness.

…setting the scene nicely for what was to come. That steep cliff, and its 199 steps, the Church Stairs, which gradually reveal more and more of the attractive red pantiled town below, lead to what must be one of the most atmospheric graveyards in the land – even on a sunny, blue-sky day the consecrated space around St Mary's looks, and feels, foggy. Add to that the wrecked majesty of the Abbey, which looms above the church and its serried ranks of crooked tombs standing sentinel high above the thrashing sea, and you have the perfect landscape in which to set a horror story of uncanny and eerily tangible atmosphere. Here it was that Lucy Westenra was attacked by the Count. Mina Murray – whose experiences are central to the novel – records in her diary:

> Right over the town is the ruin of Whitby Abbey, which was sacked by the Danes, and which is the scene of part

of 'Marmion', where the girl was built up in the wall. It is a most noble ruin, of immense size, and full of beautiful and romantic bits; there is a legend that a white lady is seen in one of the windows.

Stoker plundered the inscriptions on the church gravestones for names to use in the book – literary grave-robbing.

The Abbey Ruins

* That said, *Dracula* was one of only five of Stoker's eleven novels that could be described thus.

Workers at Charles Roberts & Co. around 1910.

David Storey (1933–2017)

The essence of true friendship is to make allowance for another's little lapses.

David Storey

David Storey was born in Wakefield, and grew up in a council house the son of a veteran coal miner, Frank Richmond Storey, and Lily (née Cartwright) Storey. He was educated at Queen Elizabeth Grammar School in Wakefield and went on to Wakefield Art School and then the Slade School of Fine Art in London. His father was adamant he should not go to art school and told him, if he did, to finance himself. Playing rugby league for Leeds RLFC (now Leeds Rhinos) at the weekend over five years on a fourteen-year contract helped him with his fees. He earned £6 a week and wrote novels on the train as he commuted back and forth.

Storey describes to James Campbell in *The Guardian* [31 January 2004] his dichotomous life, his personal north–south divide, and the special treatment he received from Leeds RLFC to allow time for the Slade:

> It had a very poor effect on the other players who were all young coal miners – this artist swanning in for matches. At the Slade meanwhile I was seen as a bit of an oaf. I only really felt at home on the train, where the two different parts of my life came together.

Storey's first literary success came with *This Sporting Life* (1960) – six previous manuscripts were all rejected. It is a novel set in the north of England about a man, Arthur Machin, who, like the book's author, aspires to be a successful rugby league player; *This Sporting Life* was made into a successful film of the same name in 1963 by Lindsay Anderson. While Machin is not Storey, Storey reveals how the novel was inspired by an actual game he played as a teenager:

> I was in the second row, with a player who was playing out his last days. At one moment the ball was at my feet, and I realised that if I picked it up I'd get my face kicked. And I hesitated just that amount, and he didn't, and he got his face kicked. He came up with a very bloody mouth, not knowing what had happened to his teeth. He just turned to me and said: 'You cunt.' The guilt induced by that was enormous, which was what prompted me to start writing about it.

If we have any doubts about how much Storey's experience of Leeds rugby league must have informed this book – 'not only the best literary novel by a sportsman, but the only one' – then allow Caryl Phillips, who himself grew up in Leeds, to dispel them:

> [Storey is] the only author who knew what it was like to be raked and stamped on by opponents, and then patronised by the chairman over drinks in the boardroom, so only he could have written such a fiercely authentic account of the hypocrisies of British sporting life.

> [Frank Keating, *The Guardian*, 1 December 2010]

He adds:

> [This Sporting Life is] the best novel about sport I've read. That it's about working-class northern sport, with the concomitant class tension, meant it spoke to me with all the more force. Rugby league, as opposed to rugby union, is very suggestive of northern identity and spirit, something I felt as both a liberating force and a claustrophobic problem. Storey might have felt similarly.

> [*Guardian*, 31 January 2004]

In his obituary of Storey, Michael Coveney [*The Guardian*, 27 March 2017] says of Storey's paradoxical life at the Slade during the week and playing rugby for Leeds on the weekend:

> His recurring themes, on stage and page, were defined by this dual experience; and by the conflict between his roots in the north and a sense of powerful dislocation in the south, as well as feelings of guilt and atonement in family life.

Arthur Machin's town is Storey's town: characterised by 'squat rows of houses... little black hutches nailed together by those big pegs of chimneys... coal lorries parked by the coal slip, ready for the morning'. Coal is key to Storey's work. His father's forty years hacking away at the coal face were made tolerable by a dream to provide his three sons with a higher education. Mr Shaw, the father in Storey's play *In Celebration* (1969) repeats this to his sons: 'I've spent half my life making sure none of you went down that pit.'

In *Flight into Camden* (1961) Margaret, the daughter of a Yorkshire miner, tells the sad story of how she goes to live with a married art teacher in Camden Town; in the end, though, family ties and roots prove too strong and their relationship descends into bitterness. Margaret's plight recalls the pressure and guilt Storey himself had endured when he left Wakefield for London, 'leaving behind the recognisable pressures of a home town and entering into a world where you make up your own rules' [James Campbell, *Guardian*, 31 January 2004].

The Changing Room (1971) play is set in a men's changing room at a semi-professional Northern England rugby league before, during and after a game, again directed by Lindsay Anderson. It draws on Storey's rugby playing days; what it lacks in plot and character development it makes up in its treatment of male relationships. After a week of stultifying, working class labour, on Saturday the men come together for a couple of hours of unarmed combat, gore and, hopefully, glory – and male bonding. References to corrupt councils, wives with degrees and opportunities for infidelity by a partner when a team member is hospitalised – all these show how the world, Storey's Yorkshire, had changed by the early 1970s.

In 1976, Storey's *Saville* won the Booker Prize for fiction. It tells the tale of Colin Saville, a much-loved miner's son growing up in a Yorkshire mining village called Saxton, from the days of the 1930s Depression to the post-war period with all its social change. The life-defining 11-plus examination looms over Colin along with other such events no doubt familiar from Storey's own Wakefield experiences. His grammar school education gives rise to the artistic ambitions and cultural values that see him alienated from his family. 'I suppose I feel apart', he says, a sentiment that engenders conflict, both within himself and with his parents. In the end he leaves home for a new life in London.

In his *Guardian* reprise of Booker prize winners [*The Guardian*, 18 November 2008] Sam Jordison confesses how, until he had read *Saville*, he was certain that Monty Python's *Working-class Playwright* sketch (1970) had scuppered any subsequent attempts to write books in the vein of D. H. Lawrence's *Sons and Lovers*:

> Nobody who has laughed at … Terry Jones' matronly hand-wringing could again take seriously a book about a son who'd rather attain the lofty heights of poetry than work down a mine. And yet here is the 1976 Booker winner set among a South Yorkshire mining family in the late 1930s, complete with small kitchen, moaning mother and an oldest son who snubs 'yon pit' to become a writer in 'that London'.

All the more remarkable as *Saville* revisits themes by then commonplace in English literature and in Storey's own work too. Being trapped in suffocating pit towns, rugby league prowess and marital infidelity had all made an appearance in *This Sporting Life*.

The Guardian review whined 'Same Old Storey', but sales of the book confirm for us that it is a story well worth repeating.

It is not all industrial landscape. Storey provides us in *Saville* with a literary seascape. An early chapter describes how a miner takes his family to Scarborough for their annual week's holiday. Storey writes:

> When the tide was out there were wide, sandy beaches, white glistening pleasure boats and the fishing smacks. There were donkeys on the sand; a man came round each morning and we have a Punch and Judy show; there was a roundabout cranked by hand ... Pleasure boats, orchestra aboard; a man in a sailor's hat sang songs.

Storey's Punch and Judy show.

In Celebration (1969), provides another example of Storey's preoccupation with his post-war generation alienated from its own roots by the social mobility facilitated by further education and economic opportunity. The miner father who has spent his life scrabbling around underground is proud of the opportunities he has allowed his sons (to keep them from the pit face) but now sees that very education betraying the work ethic he hoped to instil in them, as his working-class sons elide into middle-class professionals.

The Contractor (1969), which is about a group of workmen erecting a wedding marquee at a posh Yorkshire house, and then taking it down again, draws on Storey's experience of doing just that in a job he had in his adolescence in Wakefield.

A Serious Man (1998) portrays a successful playwright, painter and novelist (all of which Storey, of course, was) in the throes of a personal crisis. The hero, Richard Fenchurch, a one-time successful writer in his mid-sixties just like Storey, experiences a Damascene conversion to the arts on hearing Verlaine being recited at school. Storey had the same revelation one day at school. Fenchurch, haunted by the past, revisits the northern landscapes of his earlier life, going on long walks, 'looking … for what I lost, hoping for a fire among the ashes'.

Throughout his work – novels, poetry and plays, Storey's dominant themes are family and class conflicts, social transition, alienation, sport, art, education, teaching, manual labouring, marital break-up and mental breakdown. We see them especially in *A Serious Man* and in the portrayal of the suicidal impulses of a former academic in *As It Happened* (2002).

Floods in Denby Dale Road in the 1940s.

John Ronald Reuel Tolkien (1892–1973)

Not all those who wander are lost.

J. R. R. Tolkien, *The Fellowship of the Ring*

John Tolkien was born in Bloemfontein, South Africa, to where his father, a Birmingham bank clerk, had emigrated in search of a better life. When he was four Tolkien's father died, causing his mother, now in reduced circumstances, to return to Birmingham with the two children. Tolkien won a scholarship to King Edward's School in the city and was doing well when his mother died from diabetes aged thirty-four; he was twelve, and with his young brother left a penniless orphan. The boys were cared for by a compassionate Catholic priest, a friend of the Catholic family. Tolkien won a scholarship to Oxford where he studied Middle and Old English and Old Norse. After war service, which included front-line action on the Somme, he returned to Oxford where he worked on the *New English Dictionary*.

Tolkien's first acquaintance with Yorkshire was in 1916 when he attended a course at the army's Northern Command at Farnley Park, Otley; to recuperate from trench fever sustained at the front he was sent to Brooklands Military Hospital, Hull (now the Dennison Building at the University of Hull), and then in June 1917, after visits to his wife and cousin in Harrogate, he was posted to the Humber garrison – the musketry school at Hornsea. Here, he and his wife, Edith, went on a walk in a wood near Roos on the Holderness peninsula, which was full of hemlocks. In a magical Wordsworth-type moment, Edith danced and sang; so taken by this was Tolkien that he used it as the 'landscape' for the first meeting of his mythic lovers Beren and Luthien – the story re-emerges in *The Silmarillion*. It is seen again as a poem in *The Lord of the Rings:* when the hobbits fear darkness and the Black Riders, Aragorn recites part of the story of Beren and Luthien: 'The leaves were long, the grass was green,/The hemlock-umbels tall and fair...' Edith stayed at a house that is now the Lifeboat Café in Withernsea.

The two years or so spent by Tolkien at the garrison in Easington and nearby desolate Kilnsea provided material for 'The Song of Eriol', a story about wandering mariner in *The Book of Lost Tales*. Tolkien went to Whitby twice, in 1910 and 1945, imbibing the extensive Anglo-Saxon history to be found there. This particular Yorkshire landscape and the lost villages in the vicinity like Ravenser Odd may well have made a contribution to his many *Lord of the Rings* references to the ruin and decay of a once flourishing civilisation. Days on end spent watching out for an invasion from the North Sea would have furnished a unique seascape for the soldier–writer.

Tolkien's Whitby.

Tolkien was also stationed at the Thirtle Bridge Camp near Withernsea where the officers' mess still stands, now Mona House, and a cookhouse behind it, now used as a barn. The camp was home to a staggering 1,500 soldiers.

Wetwang (also called Nindalf) in *Fellowship of the Ring* is a swamp to the south of the Emyn Muil in Middle Earth, and east of the Great River Anduin, fed by the great inland delta of the Entwash. Wetwang is, of course, a village in east Yorkshire not far from Easington, its name deriving either from the Old Norse vaett-vangr, 'field for the trial of a legal action' or, more likely, from the 'Wet Field' as opposed to the dry field at nearby Driffield.

J. R. R. Tolkien came to Leeds in 1920 with Edith and their small sons to take up the post of Reader in English Language at the University. The Thoresby Society website continues the story:

> they settled in a small terrace house, 11 St Mark's Terrace, near the University. It was dingy and dark, and the sooty air rotted the curtains and covered the baby outside in his pram with smuts! In 1924, with a third child on the way, they moved to greener, pleasanter surroundings at 2 Darnley Road, West Park, Headingley, a tall Edwardian red-brick semi next to fields.

> [http://www.thoresby.org.uk/content/people/tolkien.php]

In between St Mark's and Darnley Road the Tolkiens lived in St Michael's Road before moving to Holly Bank, both in Headingley.

Tolkien's academic work at Leeds reveals an interest in local dialect influenced by his Yorkshire environment and landscapes: as a member of the Yorkshire Dialect Society he wrote the 'Foreword' to Walter E. Haigh's *New Glossary of the Dialect of the Huddersfield District*. Here he mentions his influential 1925 edition of *Sir Gawain and the Green Knight* (ed. E. V. Gordon) in which:

> Tolkien… was charmed by the way in which words familiar to him only from the medieval poem reappeared in modern dialect speech. He gives more than a dozen examples, including the dialect verb 'dloppen., in Huddersfield 'to frighten, surprise, amaze, disgust'.

In *Sir Gawain* 'dloppen' is a verb with identical meaning.

In 1925 Tolkien returned to Oxford to take up the post of Professor of Anglo-Saxon which, along with his Merton Professorship of English Language and Literature from 1945 to 1959 and his writing, kept him busy for the rest of his working life.

Keith Waterhouse (1929–2009)

I turn over a new leaf every day. But the blots show through.

Keith Waterhouse, *Billy Liar*

Keith Waterhouse was born in industrial Hunslet, Leeds; he is, of course, best known for his novel *Billy Liar* (1959) and the subsequent John Schlesinger film featuring Hull-born actor Tom Courtenay in the part of Billy.

Industrial Leeds in the 50s.

Billy Liar, William Fisher, is a nineteen-year-old working-class incurable fantasist living with his parents in the fictional town of Stradhoughton in Yorkshire. Bored rigid by his job as a humble clerk for Shadrack & Duxbury, undertakers, Billy whiles away his time day-dreaming fantasies of life in the big city working as a comedy writer. Billy is an inveterate liar: he lies that his father is a retired naval captain/cobbler, he lies to his parents that the mother of Arthur Crabtree, Billy's best friend, has broken her leg; he is engaged to two girlfriends, and in love with a third and harps on about a job offer writing scripts in London for 'Danny Boon', a comedian. One of his fiancées, Rita, is a 'hard lass'.

Waterhouse's career started at the *Yorkshire Evening Post* but he was also a regular writer for *Punch*, the *Daily Mirror*, and the *Daily Mail*. In his early days he campaigned against the colour bar in post-war Britain, the abuses committed by the British in Kenya and the British government's murky selling of weapons to various equally murky Middle Eastern countries. No change there then.

While at the *Mirror* during a newspaper strike in 1956, he wrote his first novel, *There Is a Happy Land*, set on a Leeds housing estate and which, like *Billy Liar*, draws on his boyhood in the industrial landscape of Hunslet. The book describes, through the eleven-year-old boy's eyes, a few weeks in the life of the young boy on a council estate and in the surrounding rhubarb fields, quarries and Clerk of Works' yard that form his playground. Unusually for the day, the hero is drawn as an ordinary boy, sometimes a coward, sometimes a liar, 'hard' in his own eyes and often insecure when engaging with other people. When an eccentric man over fond of children ('Uncle Mad') moves onto the estate, the tragedy begins and is especially poignant because we watch it unfold through the eyes of the young narrator, who is unable to fully understand the significance of the terrible events happening around him. The book is further enriched because it is replete with Yorkshire slang and the evocation of his own experiences allows Waterhouse to recreate so vividly his half feral street urchins.

Street games in Halliday Street, Burmantofts, 1954. © Marc Riboud.

East Grove Street, Burmantofts 1954. © Marc Riboud.

In *City Lights – A Street Life* Keith Waterhouse tells the story of his childhood and adolescence 'in soot-blackened, tramcar-rattling Leeds. He describes wandering around the city's theatres, variety-halls and teashops, and life as a junior reporter, as well as the characters he encountered, providing a portrait of England's past'. The blurb for the book describes him as 'deeply mistrustful of grass and trees. In early childhood, he would roam the covered markets, the carillon-chiming arcades. As a youth he came to know the cinemas and the theatres'…impatient like many of his contemporaries to move 'down south'.

In an interview with *The Guardian* [14 April 2001], Waterhouse describes how his Hunslet–Leeds childhood has informed his work:

> The best guess is somewhere in a working-class Leeds childhood that, Waterhouse perceptively notes, although packed with escapism, was in fact an escape into realism. He was transfixed by the nitty gritty of Leeds life, and his recollection of his adventures around the city invest the place with the same lyrical nostalgia that Woody Allen does to his childhood New York. Fellow Leeds boy Gerald Kaufman said Waterhouse's 1994 memoir, *City Lights*, gave back to him, 'the Leeds that I loved, the Leeds that time and change had taken away'.

Waterhouse's father, Ernest, was a heavy-drinking costermonger who sold vegetables from a cart in South Leeds; he died when his son was aged three leaving him a brown suit and a ha'penny left in the pocket. The family lived in fear of the bailiffs who eventually took all of the furniture except the mattresses and a stool for his mother, Elsie, to sit on. Waterhouse, however, insists on a silver lining:

> But we were richer than the poorest because my mother had a thing about shoes. She thought shoes were respectable and boots were not – and clogs positively not. She got the shoes from the public benefit shoe company, so we were a shoe-wearing family, which was quite important.

As with near contemporary and near neighbour Richard Hoggart, education was pivotal, and the springboard to better things. Waterhouse recalls how Elsie wanted the very best for her children and how she once bought a book in French for his sister – 'I suppose she thought she would assimilate this language somehow' – and when she found Keith had aspirations to write, she bought him notebooks. Moreover, 'she got me into school a year early, aged four, because I wouldn't stop reading' [Nicholas Wroe, *Guardian*, 14 April 2001].

Like Hoggart, Waterhouse failed an early exam but, notwithstanding, at thirteen, Waterhouse won a scholarship to the local college of commerce where a science teacher, who had to teach English because of the wartime shortage of teachers, exerted a big influence. 'He would just chuck a book like Huckleberry Finn at me and say "you might like this"' [ibid.]. Normally, Waterhouse would have left school at fourteen to bring some money into the house, but Elsie allowed him to stay on an extra eighteen months. 'She wanted me "to get on", as the phrase was' he says [ibid.]. When he finally left school, he took a job as a clerk in an undertakers-cum-surveyors, auctioneers and estate agents – a scenario that re-emerges in *Billy Liar*.

Of the inspiration he got from Hunslet, Waterhouse confesses:

> Down in Nottingham there was DH Lawrence writing out of muck heaps and pits, and in London there was PG Wodehouse and the Drones club. But I was stuck in a council estate in Leeds: who would want to read about that? Then I read Dylan Thomas's stories about his adolescence, *Portrait of an Artist as a Young Dog*, which was a real eye-opener. It came as a blaze that you could write about anything, and it was up to you to bring the society you were writing about alive.
>
> [*The Guardian*, 14 April 2001]

'The jail might have been the infirmary, the infirmary might have been the jail, the town-hall might have been either, or both, or anything else', so Dickens writes in *Hard Times* of the fictional city of Coketown, based on actual industrial mill towns like Preston; a century later Keith Waterhouse's Billy Liar is just as disappointed by Stradhoughton, which is 'exactly like any other High Street in Great Britain. Woolworth's looked like Woolworth's, the Odeon looked like the Odeon, and the Stradhoughton Echo's [office] looked like a public lavatory in honest native white tile'.

Index of places

Selected bibliography

Aldrich, M. 'Aubade' by Philip Larkin, https://thegadabouttown. com/2016/12/02/aubade-by-philip-larkin/

Armitage, S. *Walking Home: A Poet's Journey*, London, 2017.

Armitage, S. *Walking Home: Travels with a Troubadour on the Pennine Way*, London, 2012.

Armitage, S. *Walking Away: A Poet's Journey*, London, 2016.

Armitage, S. *All Points North,* London, 2009.

Atkins, W. *The Moor: Lives, Landscape, Literature*, London, 2014.

Atkinson, J. C. *Forty Years in a Moorland Parish: Reminiscences and Researches in Danby in Cleveland*, Oxford, 1891.

Atkinson, J. C. *Countryman on the Moors*, Oxford, 1967. (Originally *Forty Years in a Moorland Parish: Reminiscences and Researches in Danby in Cleveland*, 1891.)

Atkinson, K. *Behind the Scenes at the Museum*, London, 1995.

Barry, P. *Contemporary British Poetry and the City*, Manchester, 2007.

Bell, Lady. *At the Works – A Study of a Manufacturing Town*, London, 1985.

Bennett, A. *Keeping On Keeping On*, London, 2016.

Bennett, A. *Untold Stories*, London, 2005.

Bennett, A. *Writing Home*, London, 1994.

Birch, D. (ed.), *The Oxford Companion to English Literature 7th ed.*, Oxford, 2009.

Bounds, P. *Orwell and Marxism: The Political and Cultural Thinking of George Orwell,* London, 2009.

Bowness, A. *Barbara Hepworth: Drawings from a Sculptor's Landscape*, Westport, CT, 1966.

Bowness, S. *Barbara Hepworth and the Yorkshire Landscape: An Anthology of Her Writings and Recollections*, Wakefield, Yorkshire Sculpture Park, 2003.

Bragg, M. *Melvyn Bragg on Class and Culture*, episode 2, BBC2, broadcast 2 March 2012.

Braine, J. *J. B. Priestley*, Littlehampton, 1978.

Briggs, A. *Victorian Cities*, London, 1963.

Brook, C. *George Gissing and Wakefield: A Novelist's Associations with his Home Town 2nd ed.* Wakefield, 1991.

Chrystal, P. *Old Middlesbrough*, Catrine, 2018.

Chrystal, P. *Haworth Timelines*, Darlington, 2018.

Chrystal, P. *Old Yorkshire Country Life*, Catrine, 2017.

Chrystal, P. *Historic England – Hull,* Stroud, 2017.

Chrystal, P. *Historic England – Leeds*, Stroud, 2017.

Chrystal, P. *Historic England – York,* Stroud, 2017.

Chrystal, P. *Hull in 50 Buildings*, Stroud, 2017.

Chrystal, P. *Leeds in 50 Buildings*, Stroud, 2016.

Chrystal, P. *The Rowntree Family of York*, Pickering, 2014.

Daiches, D. *Literary Landscapes,* New York, 1979.

Davidson, P. *The Idea of North,* London, 2016.

Drabble, M. *A Writer's Britain: Landscape in Literature*, London, 1997.

Dunn, D. (ed.). *A Rumoured City: New Poets from Hull*, Newcastle upon Tyne, 1982.

Faulkner, T. (ed.) *Northern Landscapes: Representations and Realities*, Newcastle-upon-Tyne, 2010.

Findlater, J. H. The Slum Movement in Fiction, *National Review* 35, 1900, 447–454

Gardam, J. *The Iron Coast: Notes from a Cold Country – Photographs of Yorkshire*. London. 1994.

Gooderson, D. *War! Lies! And a Packet of Fags!*, 1992. (The play was given a rehearsed reading at the London and International School of Acting in January 1992. A shortened version was broadcast on BBC Radio 4 entitled *Waste of Glory* in July 1994 and repeated in November 1995.)

Hall, E. Tony Harrison's Prometheus: A View from the Left (PDF) http://www.bu.edu/arion/files/2010/03/Hall-Harrison-Prometheus.pdf

Hartley, J. *Philip Larkin's Hull and East Yorkshire*, Hull, 1995.

Hendrix, H. *Writers' Houses and the Making of Memory*, London. 2007.

Hewitt, J. The 'Haven' and the 'Grisly Rokkes': Mary Linskill's Dangerous Landscapes and the Making of Whitby. In *Northern Landscapes: Representations and Realities*, ed. by T. Faulkner, Newcastle-upon-Tyne, 2010, p. 280.

Hibbett, R. Philip Larkin, British Culture, and Four-letter Words, *The Cambridge Quarterly*, 43, 2014, 120–138 https://academic.oup.com/camqtly/article/43/2/120/370096.

Hoggart, R. *The Uses of Literacy*, London, 1957.

Holman, B. *Woodbine Willie: An Unsung Hero of World War One*, London, 2013.

Johnson, M. *Ideas of Landscape: An Introduction*, Oxford, 2007.

Kaiser, M. Permanently Bard: Selected Poetry, *World Literature Today*, winter, 1997, p. 157.

Kidson, A. *Yorkshire People and Places: Prints and Drawings from the Harrogate Fine Art Collection*, Harrogate, 2014.

Klingender, F. D. *Art and the Industrial Revolution*, St Albans, 1947.

Larkin Trail, The http://www.thelarkintrail.co.uk/beyond-the-city-centre.php?item=trialItem_name_17

Lindberg-Seyersted, Brita. Sylvia Plath's Psychic Landscapes, *English Studies* 71, No. 6, 1990, pp. 509–522.

Linskill, M. *The Haven Under the Hill: A Novel*, Whitby, 1928.

Loewy, B. (ed.) *Letters of Dante Gabriel Rossetti to William Allingham, 1854–1870*, Cornell, 1897.

London, L. *Female Poets of the First World War – Volume 2*, 2016

Mathison, P. *Tolkien in East Yorkshire 1917–1918: An Illustrated Tour*, Sutton in Ashfield, 2012.

Mitchell, W. R. *J. B.Priestley's Yorkshire*, Clapham, 1987.

Myers, A. *Myers' Literary Guide: The North East*, Manchester, 1995.

https://www.poetryarchive.org/poet/ian-mcmillan

Pollard, A. *The Landscape of the Brontës*, London, 1988.

http://www.poemspoet.com/tony-harrison

Priestley, J. B. *English Journey*, London, 1937.

Priestley J.B. *The Other Place*, London, 1953.

Priestley, J. B. *Life International*, vol. 40 no. 5, 7 March 1966.

Rowntree, B. S. *Poverty, A Study of Town Life*, London, 1901.

Rowntree, B. S. *English Life and Leisure: A Social Study*, London, 1951.

Sagar, K. www.keithsagar.co.uk/.../hughes/ted%20hughes%20fishing%20and%20poetry.pdf

Spooner, D. Places I'll Remember – Larkin's 'Here'. *Geography* 335, 77, 1992, 134–42.

Wilson, N. *Home in British Working-Class Fiction*, Farnham, 2015.

About the author

Paul Chrystal has Classics degrees from the Universities of Hull and Southampton; he worked as a medical publisher for nearly forty years. He is the author of ninety or so books, many of which are about York and Yorkshire. He is a regular contributor to a number of history magazines, is a reviewer for 'Classics for All' and he writes for a national daily newspaper, has appeared on the BBC World Service, Radio 4's PM programme and various BBC local radio stations. He lives in York.

Some other books by Paul Chrystal:

Leeds's Military Heritage, York Industry Through Time, The Place Names of Yorkshire, Haworth Timelines, Old Yorkshire Country Life, The Rowntree Family of York, Pubs In & Around York, Roman Women, In Bed with the Ancient Greeks, Women at War in the Ancient World. For a full list see www.paulchrystal.com